CAPTAINS' LOGS
SUPPLEMENTAL

By Mark A. Altman

BXTREE

••••
Acknowledgements

For taking the time to be interviewed for this book, I'd like to thank the following people in their "order of appearance": Rick Berman, Jeri Taylor, Rene Echevarria, Michael Piller, Brent Spiner, Naren Shankar, Ron Moore, Brannon Braga, Marina Sirtis, David Carson, Adam Nimoy, Alexander Singer, Winrich Kolbe, David Livingston, Richard James, Greg Jein, John DeLancie, Jonathan Frakes, J.C. Brandy, Siddig El Fadil, Terry Farrell, Michael Dorn, Dan Curry, Patrick Stewart and Cliff Bole.

••••
Book design by Paul Nicosia
••••

First published in the UK 1994
by BOXTREE LIMITED, Broadwall House
21 Broadwall, London SE1 9PL

First published in the USA 1993 by Image Publishing

10 9 8 7 6 5 4 3 2 1

Copyright © 1993 Mark A. Altman

All rights reserved

This publication is not licensed by, nor is Boxtree or Image Publishing affiliated with, Paramount Pictures. This is a scholarly work intended to explore the history of *Star Trek*.

No photos appearing in this book are copyright Paramount Pictures.

Some photographs courtesy Foto Fantasies

ISBN: 1 85283 399 8

Printed in Finland by
Werner Söderström Oy

Except in the United States of America, this book is sold subject to the condition that it shall not, by way of trade or otherwise, be circulated without the publisher's prior consent in any form of binding or cover other than that in which it is published and without a similar condition being imposed on a subsequent purchaser.
A catalogue record for this book is available from The British Library.

••••

• • C O N T E N T S • •

Introduction 4

Season Six: An Overview 5

The Episodes 42

    "Times Arrow, Part II" 43

    "Realm of Fear" 47

    "Man of the People" 48

    "Relics" 50

    "Schisms" 54

    "True Q" 57

    "Rascals" 60

    "A Fistful of Datas" 62

    "The Quality of Life" 64

    "Chain of Command, Part I" 66

    "Chain of Command, Part II" 69

    "Ship in a Bottle" 71

    "Aquiel" 73

    "Face of the Enemy" 74

    "Tapestry" 78

    "Birthright, Part I" 84

    "Birthright, Part II" 88

    "Starship Mine" 92

    "Lessons" 94

    "The Chase" 95

    "Frame of Mind" 97

    "Suspicions" 98

    "Rightful Heir" 99

    "Second Chances" 100

    "Timescape" 102

    "Descent" 104

Appendix 108

• • • • •

CAPTAINS' LOGS - SUPPLEMENTAL
INTRODUCTION

It's hard to believe that with only one remaining season of STAR TREK: THE NEXT GENERA-TION, the Enterprise 1701-D has been soaring through the cosmos for over six years, a substantially more expansive journey than that of its illustrious predecessor. The original STAR TREK berthed in television drydock after only three years of boldly going where no man had gone before.

Welcome to CAPTAINS' LOGS SUPPLEMENTAL, your complete guide to the sixth season of THE NEXT GENERATION. Last year, BOXTREE introduced CAPTAIN'S LOGS: THE COMPLETE TREK VOYAGES, and the response has been overwhelming. The fans and scholars have embraced the book as the indispensable reference guide to the complete voyages of the starship Enterprise. Needless to say, we appreciate the enthusiasm which greeted that project, a personal passion of both the authors.

A lot has happened to the crew of the Enterprise since we wrapped up TREK's fifth season in the original edition. In fact, when it looked as though THE NEXT GENERATION's best years were behind it, the writers and producers responsible for making the show went on to launch the series' most daring and innovative 26 installments yet. The sixth season was rife with creative ingenuity and provocative story-telling, a hallmark of the series.

Much of the credit for STAR TREK's creative renewal can be attributed to the stewardship of Jeri Taylor, a former producer on such shows as QUINCY and JAKE & THE FATMAN. She has allowed the writers to experiment and break out of traditional formulas and themes, proving that the Enterprise still has a lot of new worlds to chart before it is decommissioned. Unfortunately, Paramount has decided that it's time to close the log books on THE NEXT GENERATION, announcing that it's time for her crew to make the leap to the big screen where they will continue their voyages on a bi-annual basis beginning in December of 1994.

The STAR TREK universe won't remain unexplored on television, however, as DEEP SPACE NINE continues to chart new nooks and crannies of the galaxy in general and the Gamma quadrant in particu-lar. With each subsequent episode DEEP SPACE continues to improve, proving it may yet become the best TREK of all. As a result, we found the need to explore that station's voyages in yet another volume. Eschewing the CAPTAIN'S LOGS moniker, or even COMMANDER'S LOGS, we encourage you to check with your local bookseller, to pick up THE DEEP SPACE COMPANION to immerse yourself in that equally entertaining outpost on the edge of the galaxy with the same indepth interviews, commentary and information that can be found in the CAPTAIN'S LOGS series.

Until our next entry, live long and prosper, and keep on trekkin'.
Mark A. Altman

October 1993

• • • •
SEASON SIX
An Overview

In May 1993 it became official: THE NEXT GENERATION was making the leap to the silver screen. Ending Paramount's promo reel of upcoming product at Las Vegas' SHOWEST film exhibitor's convention, the studio announced the TREK feature for December of 1994 with great fanfare. Although they didn't make the announcement until August of 1993, the seventh season of TNG would be its last on the small screen.

The announcement of the first NEXT GENERATION feature film follows on the heels of one of the show's most successful seasons both in terms of increasing viewership and quality. "I've been delighted with the episodes of NEXT GENERATION this season," said series Executive Producer Rick Berman. "I've been very surprised at the ratings. They continue to get better every single year."

A lot of the credit for the creative flowering of the series in its sixth season can be given to Co-Executive Producer Jeri Taylor, who was promoted from Supervising Producer at the end of last season. Taylor, a veteran television writer/producer, ran the

Left-Right: Producer Brannon Braga, Script Supervisor Lolita Fatjo and Producer Ron Moore.

writing staff on a day-to-day basis for Executive Producer Michael Piller and Rick Berman while they devoted much of their time to launching the TREK spin-off, DEEP SPACE NINE. "I think Jeri cannot get enough praise for what she has done," said Berman. "She has a writing staff — Ron and Brannon, Rene and Naren — who have a great bond with her and they've worked together beautifully, turning out some great episodes of television. I've been able to step back to some degree from THE NEXT GENERATION because of my confidence in these people."

Taylor, who ran the staff of four writers comprised of Producer Ronald D. Moore, Story Editor Brannon Braga and Staff Writers Rene Echevarria and Naren Shankar,

was not the only one to shape the show in its sixth year. Other promotions included Merri Howard to Line Producer, assuming many of David Livingston's responsibilities for producing the series when he was elevated to Supervising Producer of both shows; and J.P. Farrell, one of NEXT GENERATION's film editors, who was promoted to the new position of Supervising Editor, fulfilling many of Berman's former responsibilities on the show.

Although Berman and Piller have distanced themselves from the day-to-day involvement that has characterized their respective tenures on the show, both have continued to oversee the work on NEXT GENERATION and their presence has continued to be felt by all departments. For

• • • •

Jeri Taylor took over the creative reigns of The Next Generation *during the sixth season, replacing Michael Piller as executive producer as Piller moved over to* Deep Space.

Taylor, the sixth season was an arduous, but rewarding year — although far more challenging than she ever expected.

"It was a thousand times worse than I could have imagined," said Taylor. "I don't think 'exciting' is the word I would use to characterize it, but now that the last show of the season has been written, I have begun to relax a little bit. It simply felt overwhelming. Michael kept coming in and saying, 'You know, this must feel very creative to you,' and I would say, 'No, it doesn't. It feels like a lot of stress and pressure and anxiety.' It was very difficult."

Taylor's job was complicated by a notable lack of producible premises existing in development. "I looked at the script status report and thought, 'How will we ever do 26?'" Taylor mused. "We had four ideas and beyond that was an abyss. I didn't stop feeling that way until 'Descent' was on stage, but I learned to roll with it and realized that the staff really was coming through. Ron and Brannon grew immeasurably as writers this year, and as my right-hand people. Rene has developed steadily to become just as much of a heavy-hitter, which has been really gratifying for me to see. Naren is more of a newcomer and he hasn't been here the whole season, but shows enormous promise."

Piller nonetheless remains the last stop before a story for THE NEXT GENERATION reaches great bird Rick Berman's desk.

"We take pitches and come up with story ideas and we run them by Jeri," said Story Editor Rene Echevarria. "She has us write it up and we send them over to Michael and he decides what stories we put into development. Then Jeri will decide whether to use the writer who pitched the story or which one of us will write the drafts of a document which will then go to Michael, and he'll ask for some changes and then it will go to Rick. If Rick approves it, we break the story without Michael and he comes in at the end and either approves it or asks for some changes and then it goes to script and he gives notes. Michael hasn't been doing any rewriting on NEXT GENERATION. That's Jeri's job now. She polishes everything. Jeri's hand is in all of these scripts, some much more than others."

For Piller, who was openly critical of the fifth season of NEXT GENERATION, Taylor's tenure has resulted in a creative renewal of which he heartily approved. "There's no question in my mind that the sixth season was far superior to the fifth season," said Piller. "I believe that we've taken more risks, we've expanded several characters in fundamental ways. We've taken care of some way overdue issues that needed to be addressed; a Geordi love story as well as finding some really wonderful things for Data, who we felt we had been cheating a little the last few years. We also felt at the beginning of the season that we had a franchise that had wonderful opportunities for fun and we rarely took them. I think there are some wonderful episodes that don't take themselves so seriously that are nice breaths of fresh air, counterbalanced by episodes that take themselves terribly seriously and are some of the great television shows of the season."

Piller traced the show's revitalization to its previous year. "I fundamentally believe this happened at the end of last season," he stated. "If you look at shows like 'Inner Light' and 'The Outcast', you will begin to see a restart of serious creativity in the NEXT GENERATION. I think essentially what you see the result of is the development of DEEP SPACE NINE. DS9 suddenly stoked the creative fires in a very constructive way. I concentrated on communicating that there was not an us and them situation; that these were all people working on STAR TREK, all in the same building, and we should help

each other and contribute to the other's show and learn about each other's show and help the universe grow. What did come however was an attitude that we have to be on our toes because there is a parallel development going on, and whatever they're doing on that show over there, I have to be doing just as well over here. So it became a very healthy situation as far as I'm concerned.

"I think we had a better mix this season than certainly the fifth season and I think its comparable to the fourth season," added Piller. "I have enjoyed THE NEXT GENERATION and I've enjoyed watching the show this year. A measurement of the success of this season is that the Enterprise has not broken down once. That's a measure of how creative the storytelling has been. As a result, I would bet that there was a 35% reduction in technobabble. The actors would tell you that. They used to call it Piller-filler, which is unfair since I know less about technology than anybody. The truth is there has been less Piller-filler this year. Maybe it's because I'm not there."

Noted actor Brent Spiner, who along with LeVar Burton has probably spoken the largest share of TREK mumbo-science, "That was one of my big complaints start-

ing with the third season. Gene [Roddenberry] always said technobabble should be used as a spice and not as the main course, and I think they've gotten back to that."

One of the reasons is that STAR TREK was avoiding the cliched jeopardy plots in its A/B story plotting, which had typified the fifth season. The A/B story usually was dual plot development comprised of a personal story coupled with a ship in peril plot, that often had nothing to do with each other. In such episodes as "Cost of Living," in which Mrs. Troi comes aboard and plays surrogate mom to Alexander, the ship is also jeopardized by a mysterious oozing organism. Sometimes these plots worked more effectively than others — as in "Silicon Avatar" which blended the story of the hunt for the crystalline entity with a vengeful mother's sorrow over the loss of her son to that destructive force — but most of the time they seemed forced. A priority for sixth season was abandoning such types of storytelling.

"It was a conscious effort to try to break away from a kind of story that seemed to have become formulaic," said Jeri Taylor. "Every week the ship was in jeopardy from this, that, or the other thing. There was a cer-

Naren Shankar, **Next Generation's** *Science Advisor and Story Editor.*

tain staleness that I think was just beginning to creep in. I don't think it was a real problem, but we definitely knew that we wanted to rejuvenate things and take some chances. If you can't take chances in the sixth or seventh season of a show, when can you do it? The show is very solid and very strong and so it's time to kind of push the edges a little bit. And we did that."

Naren Shankar, who served as the show's science advisor and became a staff writer the sixth year, was often charged with devising much of the menacing sci-fi contrivances. "The reason we got away from that format was because most everybody on the

staff didn't feel it worked," he said. "When we went to an A/B story where A was a character line and B was a straight ship jeopardy, the two didn't overlap. They're not interesting. It's just not generally a good way to tell a story. There are exceptions, 'Hollow Pursuits' was a straight A/B storyline and it was still a good episode because the B story was de-emphasized tremendously. What happens is you end up in this awkward position where in Act 5 you're just dashing to the finish. It's like get the ship in jeopardy in Act 4 and solve the character story and the jeopardy in Act 5 and let's do it and get it over with. You want things to go along in a more organic way. It's more interesting and less artificial, and everybody understands that."

As a result, STAR TREK looked towards new avenues for exploration and the show became more daring and provocative, often breaking its traditional format and dealing with more controversial issues. "It was conscious," said Michael Piller. "From the beginning of the season we said let's take more chances. One of the problems in the fifth season was we said, 'Okay, it's not a great story but we need another story for this week so let's keep going', and I think we said let's wake up and see how far out we

can go this year. We have some episodes that are as far out as any you've ever seen on this show."

"I can give a lot of credit for that to the staff," added Jeri Taylor. "I just think these four guys are absolutely wonderful. They are brilliant, contentious, creative people who keep me hopping and it's a very exciting thing to be in a room with all of them when ideas and arguments are bouncing around. It gets very heated at times, but we come up with some very, very unusual kinds of things because it's a free room, and dissent is allowed and encouraged. From that I think we hammer out things that you could never get to by taking the safe formulaic approach."

Said Michael Piller, "I've made some suggestions, I've killed a few things that I thought weren't right, I've given notes on scripts and in one particular case I turned a show inside out ['Suspicions'], but most of it has really been in Jeri's office. She deserves so much of the credit. Ron Moore has turned into a really strong writer/producer who is a leader in that room, has strong opinions and generally knows STAR TREK and how to make it work. Brannon Braga is one of the great success stories of the last several years I've been here. This is a guy who came out of the Television Academy's intern program as raw and inexperienced as you'll ever find with anybody, and has grown each year. Now he's turning in some of the most interesting work you'll ever see. I have great respect for his work and I think he will become recognized as one of the very special writers in television. Then we brought in Rene Echevarria, who had done such wonderful work for us on a freelance basis but didn't seem to do too well under pressure in the earlier years. But his work and attitude had matured and we felt he was really a good candidate to be a future staff member, and he's done a fine job. And Naren Shankar, who had been our technical consultant and also been a Writer's Guild intern, was someone else Jeri felt strongly had the potential to make a significant addition. We brought him in mid-season. This is a staff that's ticking like a watch. It's doing a wonderful job. If I had any credit to take at all it was helping these people to know what works and what doesn't over the last three years."

Despite a willingness to explore bold new themes, not every idea made it to the screen. Some concepts were just too outlandish — even for the out-of-this world series. "Last year we wanted to make

Geordi an alien," recalled Jeri Taylor. "He was going to discover that his father was not who he thought he was and his mother had an almost ROSEMARY'S BABY-kind of thing and been impregnated by an alien. As a result, Geordi was actually half alien and now, at his present age, his people were coming back to get him. I thought that would have given Geordi's character a lot of elaboration."

Another more recent idea was the staff's enthusiasm over actually killing Commander Riker in "Second Chances," an episode in which the Enterprise discovers a duplicate of Riker that was created in a transporter malfunction on an Away Team mission nearly a decade earlier.

"Our Lieutenant Riker didn't make it," said Taylor. "Maybe we were trying to rock the boat a little too drastically. My original idea, which we thought was very bold and surprising and would energize the seventh season, was to kill our Commander Riker and let Lieutenant Riker come onto the ship as a rejuvenated, energetic, driven, ambitious Lieutenant. He wouldn't be Number One, he would be at ops and have to prove himself and build his career and get into conflict with the others because he had these rough edges from having lived that

arduous experience. It gave it a wonderful life that would energize the seventh season with everyone in different places and a new character, and yet our same character was there. I was very, very taken with that. It was just too bold."

"That was one I basically said no to," explained Rick Berman. "But it gave me a lot of pause. My initial kneejerk reaction was no and then I became a little bit more willing to say yes, but there were other problems it created. Once I started leaning towards yes, we started looking at what that would do and how it would fit into the movies and how it would fit into a lot of the different relationships. Basically, you're putting a character on the ship who has not experienced anything of the last six years and doesn't know any of the characters. How would it affect the movie and other variables? I ended up feeling rather strongly that I didn't want to kill off Riker and I didn't get any major arguments about it from Michael or Jeri."

"It's a fascinating premise," said Michael Piller. "The most interesting part of it is Older Riker vs. Younger Riker and that changed along the way since they were the same age. I had two very strong feelings about this story. The premise of this was that this was going to be the season cliffhanger and that the new Riker would come onboard and during the course of the episode the Riker we've come to know and love would be killed and the young Riker would take his place as a Lieutenant on the ship next season. Rick and I both did not like this idea, Rick more than I. Riker has always been a difficult character for writers to write and they said `Let's get some conflict, let's get some excitement and energy,' but the fact is he's a pretty darn good character. A character that I relate to a great deal. When I came into the room and I read the story, I said everything about this story suggests that the new Riker comes onboard and he's everything that the old Riker's lost. I resent that as somebody wrote in the 'Best of Both Worlds' that he's come to a place in his life where he appreciates what he has and comfortable with his friends and has achieved a great inner peace. I don't believe that the guy who is a loose-end six years ago is necessarily the good part of the man. I fought very hard to protect the Riker that we had on the ship. I think the scenes between Riker and Troi are wonderful and answers a call from the fans that has existed for a long time to put those two back together again and, of course, I came up with the

final twist at the end which is that instead of, as was originally written, that he dies, we keep him alive and send him off to who knows where because what other show could ever do that? Everybody in the audience is going to expect him to die."

This year, Ron Moore, who has contributed some of the show's best teleplays since he was brought on staff during third season, has noticed a very different tenor to the staff's break sessions, where stories are plotted out on a large dry-erase board by the staff to serve as the conceptual template for writing the teleplay.

"What happened was Jeri got more involved and she made a decision early on to introduce a little more fun and a little more humor into the show this year, and we sort of ran with that," said Moore. "I think Jeri encourages a great deal of a dissent and argument in meetings. Michael's very open about things that happen in meetings and the direction of the show, but Jeri almost encourages people to take opposing points of view and really pushes the sort of philosophy of progress through dissent. You know, she really goes a little further in that direction than Michael does."

Story Editor Brannon Braga, who was promoted to Co-Producer for the seventh

season, agreed. "If I had to say one thing changed, it's probably the break sessions, which is the real meat and potatoes of script development. No offense to Michael, he has a brilliant story structure sense, but he tends to run those sessions. He's open to input and he's open to discussion, but it was much more of a monarchy when he was in the break session. Now it's more of a diplomacy. The break sessions often take two or three times as long now as opposed to when we were with Mike, who was brisk, had a vision of the show and could guide us through it. In the end, I find our break sessions a little more rewarding, we discuss things more and have more philosophical discussions. In the end, I find break sessions a little more rewarding. I think that for the most part the shows this year work although sometimes they don't. If nothing else, they have been eclectic and very creative. We're trying new things."

In musing over Braga's comments Piller remarked, "I think people got used to looking at me in the chair and seeing what I wanted to do and if I didn't know what else to do, the ship would break down," said the producer. "Now in their court they have the opportunity and the responsibility of being creative to solve the problems. Jeri and Ron and Brannon have found new stories to tell and have taken chances. When I looked at the story the first time, I would say go try it and they would come back in with something marvelous. It's their initiative. I'm proud of them for being able to do it."

One of the most difficult breaks, Naren Shankar recalled, was for Part II of "Birthright", in which Worf discovers prisoners of the Khitomer Massacre who have stayed voluntarily in a Romulan prison camp.

"Part One of the break was easier, but in Part II there were disagreements about the conception of how this particular microcosm of society had evolved," said Shankar. "Ron and I were saying that the camp had gone one way and these people were guards who just held onto the trappings of being guards and that these other people are still prisoners. Others were saying there's still a division and still other people said there are no guards anymore. It just went round and round, but the problems centered around the philosophical underpinnings of this society. We couldn't go on without resolving them and if we did we would have ended up with a mish-mash of things that didn't make any sense. Jeri Taylor, bless her heart, always let's us go, but she'll

always be the one at the end who says, 'Okay, this way,' but she does that as a last resort. She gives us very free reign."

Brent Spiner, who had been somewhat critical of the previous season, was effusive in his praise of the writing staff's talent and accessibility. "They're not defensive," he said. "They really want to hear what you have to say and I found myself calling them to say 'great work' more often than I usually do because it really was."

It's an opinion echoed by actress Marina Sirtis. "In my opinion, if it isn't the best season, it's close to it," she said. "I think we've had some really good episodes. I don't think we've had as many dull episodes as sometimes we've had in the past; 'Justice', 'Angel One'. I think, for me, it's been the best season yet."

In fact, in many ways this past year seemed like too completely different seasons. It year began with part two of "Time's Arrow", in which Mark Twain is inadvertently sent into the future and tours the Enterprise. It was followed by several heavy high-concept science-fiction episodes, including "Realm of Fear", in which Barclay encounters creatures in the transporter; "Man of the People", where Troi becomes a receptacle for the negative emotions of a

conflict mediator; and "A Fistful Of Data's", in which the holodeck malfunctions and results in a deadly Data gunfighter facing off against Worf in the center of a computer-generated town. With "Chain of Command", a dark and conflict-ridden two-parter, the season appeared to make a dramatic departure in tone and substance.

"It's a very interesting insight, and not one I probably would have made," said Jeri Taylor. "To say there is an overall design which 'Chain of Command' heralded in tone is not inaccurate, but it was not intentional. We did want to go with some sci-fi, high-concept stories, sort of offbeat, bizarre things. And then after that it was a matter of what do we have here?"

"I agree that it's a more ambitious season," said Brannon Braga. "The production staff is going a little crazy because each show is so different and that's the fun thing about this year. Ambitious is the key word. I think we've really tried to do some interesting stories. Mid-season seemed to signal that we were getting antsy and the high-concept wasn't enough. I think its serendipitous. Certainly getting to write 'Birthright' was great for me, because after doing a string of high-concept action shows — which is what

I like to do — it was really nice to do something with more profound elements. Observations of a shift are true. Why it happened is serependity. I think Rene is the only one who thinks the beginning of the season really sucked. I think the shows are a nifty, eclectic mix and I have no qualms at all about the beginning of the season. We were all very happy about it."

Offered Brent Spiner, "I do think 'Chain of Command' was sort of a turning point in the season, even though there were some good episodes prior to it. From what I've read and heard from them, the way the season started off, fans thought we were going to have a dud season and something happened about midway through and everything turned around. From that point on almost every episode was top notch. I wish 'A Fistful Of Datas' had come later in the season, because it's sort of attached to the early batch where it seemed the new writers were trying to find their way with it. Once they clicked in, every week was an exciting episode and something worth watching."

Naren Shankar agreed that the shift was more attributable to happenstance than a conscious decision by the staff to tackle bigger issues. "It may simply be we ran out of high-concept and had to dig deeper," he said. "It did change the tone for the rest of the season."

"I'm very happy with the season," opined Ron Moore. "There were some moments when I was wondering if we were doing our best work and then, at about 'Chain of Command', it just all came together and the last half of the season is very strong with a real good punch to it. Every year I see the same stuff on the computer bulletin boards. Every year they start out the same way after four episodes, posting messages like 'This season sucks. Last season was the best season ever and this year sucks.' And somewhere about the fourth episode of the seventh season the revisionism will now declare the sixth season to be the greatest season ever done on the show."

Other concerns revolved around the future of the show as well with rumors running rampant that Patrick Stewart would not be returning for a seventh year.

"There was concern, but I think we all felt they were going to do features and that was a big carrot to get him to commit to another year," said one member of the writing staff. "When we were doing 'Chain of Command', that's when the first inkling that Patrick might not be coming back was heard. Bringing in a new captain in Part One, you could see how that could give the show a really fresh start if you could find somebody good. Frankly, we were more concerned that Brent wasn't going to come back, because Brent is irreplaceable. You don't just bring on another android or cart out a Vulcan or something to fill his role. You have to have a captain and there was, in fact, some enthusiasm about the possibility of getting someone new. We were talking about bringing a woman in."

While shooting the pilot for DEEP SPACE NINE, veteran TREK director David Carson considered the possibility of Stewart leaving.

"I believe the show is not about a star and not about a Captain Kirk or a Jean Luc Picard," he noted. "I think there will inevitably be some sort of shake-up, as there always is when a captain leaves a ship, and there will be a feeling of the ground. But you may find that you get a different, richer NEXT GENERATION out of it and you're not simply retreading the same waters with the same people. The regrouping of the cast and the realignment of the actors towards either new people or redistribution of their own strengths, will inevitably make NEXT GENERATION different."

Said Jeri Taylor, "As far

as I know, that was completely informal. There were for thirty minutes or so some real concerns Patrick wouldn't be back. Most of the people felt in all probability he *would* be back. The negotiations were difficult and had he not come back then the door would have been wide open."

The idea towards focusing more on science-fiction storytelling had been a priority for the staff ever since the end of the previous season. Fifth year's "Violations", in which alien telepaths were accused of mind rape, served as the template for developing new, high-concept science-fiction stories which blended character drama with a "neat sci-fi gag," as the staff often refers to their high-concepts. Ultimately, after a few episodes early in the season, the well ran dry, thus requiring a new approach which was probably for the best.

"To some degree it's a valid assessment," said Michael Piller. "I would say the high-concept science-fiction stories that dominated the beginning of this season were the result of feeling that we had not been doing very good science-fiction fifth season. When I said we want to have more fun with it, I said let's go out there and see what we can do with setting up some challenges for ourselves in the sci-ence-fiction area as well."

The problem to any TREK director after six years of episodes is finding a new angle or shot aboard the Enterprise. "You're always looking for something new to do," said freshman TREK director Adam Nimoy. "If I see something that I like, I'm going to use it again. It never looks the same twice. I mean, ideally, you want to put your own vision on it, but the bridge has been shot from every which way, so there is not a whole lot that's new on there, but still you try to make interesting shots, and hopefully it looks a little different from something else that you've seen. My ideal way of story telling is being as simple as possible and just playing to what the drama is all about, so if I can find something that is interesting and it serves the scene, then I feel content — even if it is something that somebody has done before a thousand times."

Another first-time STAR TREK director is veteran helmer, Alexander Singer. Among his directing credits are the original MISSION: IMPOSSIBLE, IN THE HEAT OF THE NIGHT and QUINCY, as well as several features. Yet few television shows have provided him with the excitement of shooting STAR TREK.

"One of the first magazines I read was THRILLING WONDER STORIES, and there was a story called 'Hollywood on the Moon'. There was a pop art picture of a spaceship on the moon with a movie crew shooting a picture, and I couldn't wait. My love for the fantastic has very rarely had an opportunity to jive with my screen directing career. STAR TREK was one of the rare exceptions where science-fiction and film had some intersection."

Singer, who went to high school with Stanley Kubrick, said "Twenty or thirty years ago when I first began to direct, I felt that most science-fiction films were hopelessly child-like. I was living in the time that eventually happened when Lucas did STAR WARS and Kubrick did 2001. That's what I expected from science-fiction and I have a passion as a layman for the sciences and particularly astronomy. It was all very personal and means a great deal to me as it's a life-long interest."

Although the writing staff began the season with several premises already in the pipeline, many early setbacks made it difficult to stay ahead of the production buzzsaw. While spared the rampant rewriting which even took place during post-production of the first season — looping new dialogue over the completed episodes — and the

Mark Twain played an integral role in "Time's Arrow" parts one and two.

frenzy that typified Michael Piller's first year on the show, where he initiated a dramatic departure in terms of storytelling as well as clashes among the diverse personalities assembled on the show, sixth year posed its own unique dilemmas — although personal conflicts were not among them for once.

"There *has* been time pressure," said Brannon Braga. "There's been teleplays I've had a week to write. I had a week to write 'Timescape', which is fine. A lot of good stuff comes out of pressure."

Unfortunately the time pressures this season were intensified by several early problem-plagued scripts, many of which never made it to the screen. Among them were a Q script eventually vetoed by Piller, which made the rounds of practically every writer on the staff, and an Ensign Ro script that was killed when Michelle Forbes chose not to continue onboard the Enterprise, even after having refused a starring role on DEEP SPACE NINE.

"The Q show hurt us pretty bad," said Brannon Braga. "So did "Rascals", which was the first show we broke last season. We had to break it three times because Michael was not happy with it."

The problems began with protracted discussions regarding the conclusion of Data's time trek in "Time's Arrow", the fifth season cliffhanger in which Data's head is found in a cave sealed for hundreds of years on earth.

"Once again, we had developed the first part of the cliffhanger without a clue as to what would happen in the second part, which can be an exciting way to work," said Jeri Taylor. "You paint yourself into a corner and you're forced to be very creative in order to get yourself out. This one was a nightmare. When you deal with time travel I can't tell you how complicated it gets to try to figure out what to do — and arguments and discussions about different time lines and alternate universes. It was just awful to try to get the story going. Even when we finally went to script, we kept changing the story so it was a matter of going back and wrenching out sections and restructuring and plugging in other things and then taking all that away again. It was probably the most troubled episode of the year."

Said Brannon Braga, "We all feel like we know how time travel works — and it's an imaginary concept. Ron has his conception and Jeri has hers and I have mine and it's a matter of consolidating all of those ideas. The conversations would frequently descend into bizarre, ludicrous realms of time theory, which will frequently happen on this show. You have to keep in perspective that what you're talking about is imaginary, but at the same time as a staff it's our ability to be able to imagine things like time travel as real phenomenon so completely that we believe it. That gives us the ability to write the show. There have been writers on the show who didn't believe and they didn't work because they could never get it. I think you have to be a little bit schizophrenic to be able to embrace unreal concepts as reality and explore them."

The first part of "Time's Arrow" had also been considered difficult to understand by many viewers, which made writing the resolution even more difficult. "We were trying to figure out how to wrap it up and make it clear, but the aliens were confusing, the time travel was confusing and what the aliens were up to was not clear," said Taylor. "It was just a technical kind of nightmare. That was like the kickoff to the year, and by the time I was finished with that, I was just ragged and exhausted and I thought, 'Oh God, how will I ever get through this year?'"

Said Echevarria, "I'm not sure people knew enough in Part One. We just disappeared into a big wall of light. Where are we going? Did anybody know? It was pretty tightly wrapped up, though. It was fun to see our people in those outfits and it looked great with horses and carriages and locations."

"I participated on this a little bit," said Michael Piller. "I thought the scene where Sam Clemmens comes to the Enterprise and was walked around by Troi was a chance to restate the goals and vision that Roddenberry started with. I thought that was a wonderful scene and Whoopi did a great job with the show. It was colorful and it was fun. It was very complicated and time shows are very difficult. I thought the resolution was nicely handled."

By the time the dilemmas revolving around "Time's Arrow II" were resolved, other difficulties arose, including the continuing struggle to complete "Q Makes Two," a story which the staff continued to wrestle with in the hopes of creating a Q vehicle in the aftermath of a Q-less season the previous year. In the show, Q creates a duplicate of the Enterprise to prove to Picard that humans still have a dark side, which they only suppress.

"We wasted an enormous amount of time with that Q show of mine," said Echevarria, who had been handed the rewrite as his first job on staff. "We broke it three of four times. It was odd, I got here and we had five or six approved stories which Mike and Rick both signed off on and we were in the best position we'd ever been in starting a season. But 'Time's Arrow' dribbled away a huge amount of time after having been broken three or four times, and my Q show took more time. Then having episodes that had to fill certain slots rather than being able to put them where you want them.... before you know it, you're in a terrible situation."

Several logistical problems arose early in the season as well, resulting in the need for "Relics" to be pushed back on the production schedule due to Jimmy Doohan's availability to reprise his Scotty role, plus a window that opened up in Whoopi Goldberg's tight availability schedule. The delay in "Relics", whose script was ready to go to stage, necessitated rushing another script into prep which didn't allow for the usual development process. As a result, "Man of the People" was born.

"This was probably the low point of the year and since it came so early it did a lot to sort of color my dire feelings that I was not going to be alive by the end of the season," said Jeri Taylor. "We went through months of developing different kinds of ideas for 'Q Makes Two', creating traits that one would have and traits the Q duplicates would have and justifying it. We finally thought we had an okay way to go and Michael had approved it and Rene sat down and started writing the script. And I thought, 'Oh, this is not working, we're in trouble here.' I took a crack at it, and we kind of gave it all to Michael and Michael said, 'None of this is working,' and he was absolutely right. I remember the morning he called me in and said this just isn't working, but we didn't have anything else. We're never in that position where we have *nothing*. We usually have three or four other things — or least one other thing to fall back on."

"It actually was what we call a rainbow script," said director Winrich Kolbe. "It means every change is a different color and you keep getting pages in different colors the night before, sometimes the same morning that you're shooting and sometimes even in the afternoon. The general gist of the story stayed the same and that's the important thing for me. People have a tendency at times to believe if they don't change a location or a set or change actors completely around in a script revision that internal scene changes don't really matter that much, but to me they do because they affect my staging. They affect the timing of a scene. They affect my work with the actors. And so, basically, that means the moment I get those pages I have to read-dress myself the night before and redo it at times."

The biggest dilemma for Kolbe was photographing Marina Sirtis, whose transformation into a aging, jealous shrew as the result of becoming the receptacle for an ambassador's negative emotions, involved time-consuming prosthetic applications which made it difficult for the director to schedule.

"The show was a logistical nightmare because you could only do one change a day," said Kolbe. "When we had scenes where she popped up at a different age in the same location, we could not shoot that location the same day. We could not shoot her quarters, for instance, or the guest quarters, all in one fell swoop. We had to shoot the scene with her in a particular makeup and then move to another set or another stage and either pick it up the next day or come back the same day about three or four hours later and continue shooting it there. It was not the easiest way of doing a show. That's something that happens quite

frequently when you have makeup changes. Later on I did the show 'Birthright I', where we had a similar problem where Data was Data and then Data also was Dr. Soong."

"Man of the People" was a story the staff had bought on a pitch taken by new Supervising Producer Frank Abatemarco. "But he hadn't even started on it and prep was four days away on the episode," said Taylor. "So we did our first gang-bang. We parceled it out, each of us took an act, and had a day to do that and after a day we had a script. It was sort of like the elephant built by blind men. Each act had a different flavor, a different approach and a different writing style and it was really a mess. Then we just kind of had to beat it until it got hammered out — so that was one of those no sleep, panic kind of situations."

Abatemarco, who left the show when the option on his contract wasn't renewed after several months on staff, had been brought aboard during the summer hiatus by Piller. The writer/producer, who had worked on such shows as SIMON & SIMON, had been hired for a variety of reasons — most of all to give support to Taylor, who Berman and Piller were unsure would be able to get through the season on her own.

"Very simply, Jeri was going into the season with a bunch of young people and Ron and Brannon had not been asked to step up and take responsibilities that they have evolved into. I wanted to give her someone strong so she didn't feel like she was out there alone," said Michael Piller. "Frank had been pitched to us for a number of years and I sat down and had lunch with him and I was just terribly impressed with his philosophy. I said to Jeri, 'I know you're going to hate me for saying this, but go have lunch with the guy and see what you think.'"

Abatemarco had never written a STAR TREK script, and the fact that they were willing to risk hiring someone who hadn't completed a teleplay on the series (thus breaking their own stringent rules against untried TREK scribes) was indicative of the concern Piller and Berman had going into the season. "He and I got along very well," said Taylor of Abatemarco, who refused to comment through his agent. "I liked him. I wished it worked out and it didn't."

"The hardest thing there is in this business is to find people who can write STAR TREK," said Michael Piller. "Frank Abatemarco is a terrific writer and he's done a lot of wonderful work in this town but as so often happens when we hire a writer without trying him out on a script first, it has not worked out and forced us into this situation. Frank was not getting to the bottom of the characters, it was just not reading like STAR TREK. We tried to give him feedback. Jeri was working with him far more than I was, but the bottom line was he wasn't getting done what needed to get done and so we just decided to go separate ways. He left with a great deal of bitterness and there was a very uncomfortable scene between him and I before he left. I regret that because I still respect his work and it's just a shame. But it was something Jeri felt very strongly about and I backed Jeri up 100%"

Added Brannon Braga, "A lot of good writers don't get STAR TREK and have a difficult time with it. Frank was an intensely personable fellow and from what I've seen of his work, a superior writer. What I sensed was that he wasn't getting STAR TREK."

Ultimately, what emerged from the chaos was a troubled episode with some standout moments. "I thought it was a fascinating premise and Marina did a fabulous job," said Jeri Taylor. "If it was a flawed episode, it was far better than it deserved to be considering its troubled inception."

One of the only writers not to work on "Man of the People" was Brannon Braga, who was writing the episode that would be the second show of the season, "Realm of Fear," where Barclay evidences his transporter phobia. "It's like a lot of my shows can be," said Braga. "The first three acts are fun and then the tech gets in. I like to do mysteries and you have to explain things in Act 4 and 5 and it's difficult to tie it all up. 'Realm of Fear' had a lot of elements that were hard to consolidate. All in all it was a nice character piece."

"The explanation by the end really got painfully detailed," said Jeri Taylor of "Realm's" tech-heavy ending. "It's that fine line you try to draw. We feel that if we don't say something the audience is going to be fairly confused and feel cheated, because they don't understand it. But if we do say it, are they going to be overwhelmed by the words? We went one way in 'Time's Arrow II', and maybe we tried too hard to explain things in 'Realm of Fear.'"

Agreed Naren Shankar, "This show went a little overboard with the techno stuff. It hit that wall of impenetrability towards the end which was unfortunate because it was a very good idea. The tech got out of control. There was a lot of things going on, there was a

plasma stream, there was this autopsy that was going on in a very in-depth way and we didn't know what was going on, and there was a transporter problem and there was something in the pattern buffer, then it was something in the transporter beam and it kept getting layered on. It was hard enough keeping track of it in the script and by the time it gets to the screen, if you say a line too fast or if you're attention wanders for a minute, you're gone, you're lost, and I think that's what happened."

"We had a lot of conversations about that," said Supervising Producer David Livingston. "We had philosophical discussions about whether or not somebody was conscious during the transport process. And I get too literal sometimes in the meetings, but I had a real problem with it because what we were implying was we were going to have an effect where you go from one side and then visually see the image denigrate and then we see some kind of fuzzy area and then we come out to the other side and rematerialize. I thought that implied that somebody can see this process all the way through, and we had a long discussion on it and decided they couldn't, because your matter breaks up into whatever it breaks up into to make the transporter effect.

James Doohan, reprising his role of Scotty in "Relics", has often met with fans at various conventions held throughout the year (photo copyright © 1993 Karen Witkowski).

Ultimately, it was decided that somebody was only aware and could see the tail end of beaming out and the very beginning — just at their molecules started to coalesce. The effects that they ended up pulling off to create that were pretty cool."

Equally special-effects intensive was "Relics," which introduced Montgomery Scott to the 24th Century. With the ratings bonanza reaped by Mr. Spock's entree to the 24th Century in last season's "Unification," it seemed as though it would only be a matter of time, literally, before another classic cast character found their way to 24th Century.

The genesis of Chief Engineer Montgomery Scott's return to STAR TREK is in a pitch made by Michael Rupert, a freelance writer, who pitched a story in which a character from 80 years hence was found in a transporter loop. "The story didn't work and we didn't really like it, but the notion of someone staying alive in the transporter was a neat gimmick so we bought the premise of that technical nugget from him," said writer/producer Ronald D. Moore, explaining that it was Michael Piller who suggested using it to bring back one of the original series characters. "Everybody started to pick up their ears and we started going through who it could be. It seemed like Scotty was the best choice. We'd seen Spock and then you look around and realize Scotty was the character that you could have the most fun with, because you knew a lot about him. Sulu, Chekov and Uhura are fine characters, but they don't have a lot of the qualities Scotty did; the obsession with the engines, the drinking, and we could do a relationship between him and Geordi. He was sort of ready-made to do this kind of a show."

Originally Brannon Braga was given the assignment to write the show, but both his desire to script "A Fistful Of Datas" and Moore's affinity for the material resulted in him taking over the writing of the episode. "I asked to do it and they let me write the story," said Moore. "Rick said he would approach Jimmy about it and see if he was interested. He gave him a call and it became a go. And then I broke the story and everyone was real happy with it and we just went ahead and did it."

Said Brannon Braga, "I knew I couldn't possibly write it. I didn't even know who Scotty was. This was a Ron story and I asked that they just not give me the Q story that was going around that was the bane of everyone's existence at the time. It was Ron's show and I had little to do with it.

Ron really brought that show to life and he was the only guy who could do it justice."

In previous years, the large shadow of the original often meant shying away from references to the previous series, but in the case of "Relics", Moore, a longtime STAR TREK aficionado, was allowed to embrace it. "I think in the earlier seasons of the series we felt like this show had to go and prove itself and we made the decision very early on that we weren't going to pick up any old plot lines. We weren't going to talk about those guys and we weren't going to have their sons and daughters on the show. This was going to stand on its own. And that philosophy drove the show for quite a while. 'Sarek' was the first time that it felt comfortable enough to sort of start to acknowledge its history a little more and then after 'Unification', I think they sort of felt, 'Well, okay, that wasn't so bad, we can do this without really destroying who we are and we can do shows that make references to the old series without destroying our own.' So when 'Relics' came around, there wasn't a big cry and debate about it."

Said Michael Piller, "One of the great things about 'Relics' is that it wasn't a Scotty show. It was a concept about an engineer or a captain being caught in a transporter beam that we come upon as we do in the show, and I suggested it be Scotty. I thought we were going to have a problem with Mr. Berman, who generally doesn't like to do that gag. Oddly enough, he was in a good mood that day. Rick has opened his mind in a lot of ways. When I came onboard you could not mention the old STAR TREK in an episode, you couldn't make a reference to a character without major problems. When we brought Sarek onto the show it was like, 'My god, we had to march across the street and pay homage,' but now because we are firmly established I think everybody feels a lot more comfortable that we have proven ourselves. We don't owe anything to the old STAR TREK, except like the guys who went to the moon, the Mercury guys had to go up there first and we respect them for that, but we're not depending on them anymore. We don't feel we have to bend over backwards not to mention them."

"I set out to do a show that was nostalgic and sentimental and that would resonate with what people cared about," said Moore. "I got a lot of support from Jeri and Michael and Rick and they all liked the script. Rick was very supportive of the fact that it

was a sentimental and nostalgic show."

"'Unification' was a much less personal show," said staff writer Naren Shankar of last year's episode which was Spock's first appearance on THE NEXT GENERATION. "'Unification' was cast as a big geo-political situation and when you do that it becomes harder to bring out the human element because you have this huge thing happening with the Romulans trying to take over Vulcan at the expense of the personal story. 'Relics' didn't have that problem because it was, basically, about one guy. It was an intimate show and a small show in a way that Unification' was not."

With the return of Scotty approved, Moore then seized upon the idea of having the former chief engineer recreate the former Enterprise bridge on the holodeck, a moment that is one of the highlights of the episode and perhaps NEXT GENERATION. "We had Scotty and then Ron came up with this wonderful idea of recreating the old starship. It was an interesting dilemma because it was a very expensive proposition," said Piller. "It was actually cut out after the first meeting with Rick and the production people. But, that's movie magic and we sort of went around three different ways of doing it

wrong and all of us knew maybe we'd get back to the right way. We wondered if we could rent a simulation from a convention or pieces of it. Finally the tech guys came up with a way to do it. I thought that was a magical show that worked not just because Scotty was in it but because it was good idea, well executed, and well written with great special effects."

Helming his first episode of STAR TREK was veteran director Alexander Singer, who had the challenge of shooting one of TREK's most expensive and complex episodes to date. "I was very concerned about the special effects and how they would fit into a television schedule," recalled Singer. "I had never done that many special effects in a whole show riddled with these things, so that was my central question."

Another concern for the director was the condition of his guest star, actor James Doohan. "The next question was that I had never worked with Jimmy Doohan and I felt that potentially the show was a kind of classic and I understood what I had in my hands. I did not know, physically, what shape Doohan was in. There was a lot of dialogue and I don't think he ever did a show in the old STAR TREK where he had this much drama and this many notes to hit. I had seen the STAR TREK movies and I think that's still true, I don't think he ever was the center, he was always peripheral and in this episode he was the center. By the time we came to the scene on the old STAR TREK deck, he was not only the center but he had to support a very powerful dramatic scene. It's a scene that in reading it, I choked up. Part of me is very hardheaded and realistic and then part of me is very romantic and very sensitive and I was deeply moved by that story."

"It's not simply that I am also an old man retiring or an old man looking at the end of a long career," he added "It's that the concept is deeply moving. I had great sympathy for him and the things Picard was saying to him, and the evocative quality just reading the script sent chills up and down my spine. I still feel it. My wife, who watches virtually no television, has none of my sympathies and none of my interest in science-fiction, watched me shooting that scene and it made her cry."

Singer had his concerns about Doohan allayed during a meeting between him and the actor prior to shooting. "I wanted to meet him first so we didn't meet on the set. He came in graciously, we talked and his delight in doing it and

his manner reassured me enormously," said the director. "I think that he wanted me to be comfortable and he wanted me to have a sense that he could indeed carry this load, and he convinced me. And subsequently I think there was only one day, one scene, where he had a very technical page of technobabble and he was utterly exhausted at the end of a very long day, that we had any problems whatsoever. For the rest of it he was a delight to work with and he got all the jokes, so to speak."

Another concern was finding the proper balance in the relationship between Scotty and Geordi, which begins as antagonistic and eventually turns into one of mutual affection. "I think I always had an understanding that it wasn't going to destroy Geordi's character," said Ron Moore. "In a sense, Geordi was right. Who is this guy to be hanging around my engine room and giving me a hard time? As long as he played him straight and eventually made him sort of see Scotty's point of view and understand and be a little sympathetic, I knew it was going to work."

Alexander Singer was less convinced when he received the script, worrying that Geordi's dismissals of Scotty could backfire among the audience who would be

naturally sympathetic towards Doohan's character. "I had not worked with LeVar, so what I did was meet with him to talk to him about it," said Singer. "I don't think he'd done that before. I figured it's a new guy and I'd talk to him. But I think he was a little annoyed because in effect I wanted to be reassured that he understood that balance and LeVar's feeling was, 'Of course I understand it. If I don't understand this, I don't understand anything.' It turned out that LeVar is like the cast in general, some of the best actors I've ever worked with anywhere, and in the scenes it was possible to fine-tune the performance. Sometimes the guys hit the right level immediately. Sometimes we had to work for it. The combination of hostility turning into affection was very moving to me."

In writing the confrontations between Geordi and Scotty, Ron Moore had some distinct ideas about their aspirations and goals in Starfleet which defined them as two very different characters. "Scotty never wanted to be anything else but an engineer," said Moore. "He was happiest in the engine room. The ship was a living being to him. She was a lady and there was a whole different philosophy. And with Geordi, although I know he loves his job and was having a good time at it, it's not the same thing. Geordi used to be on the bridge. I'm sure he wants to command his own ship some day, like probably most engineers in the fleet do. Scotty was different and he had a different relationship."

"Scotty and Geordi are probably the two most different people you could ever imagine," said Naren Shankar, another longtime STAR TREK fan. "Ron felt very strongly about that. His point, which is arguable, is that Geordi doesn't think of himself as an engineer. Geordi is the kind of guy who when he wants to relax might go to the beach, play some classical guitar music or hang out. Scotty is the kind of guy who will go into his room and read technical manuals. Scotty is an engineer through and through and he likes to break rules and do things in an unorthodox manner. He likes to tinker and Geordi is not that way. As a result, I think it's reasonable that they clashed initially."

Although "Realm of Fear" and "Relics" were relatively trouble-free productions, the production juggernaut once again threatened to overtake the writing staff by Episode #233. Entitled "Rascals," it was the episode whose log-line made it appear as though NEXT GENERATION

was facing creative entropy. In the show; Picard, Guinan, Ro and Keiko are turned into children. Since it was one of the few premise's that involved Whoopi Goldberg, whose schedule had briefly opened up, the show was rushed into pre-production.

"The premise was an idea like 'Darmok' and 'Devil's Due' that had been around for years and gone through hundreds of rewrites," said Jeri Taylor. "Michael finally did a story on it himself last season and that's when we knew it could definitely be an episode. We gave many people we were trying out for staff positions this year a shot and it still just wasn't working. We sent 'Rascals' to Rick Berman, and he said 'You know, this is never going to make it, forget it. Why are you still beating this dead horse?' And we kept giving it to yet other writers and so it finally came to pass for show seven. We didn't have anything else. This is a prime example of how the stories drive the show. We look around and it's panic. We say 'What is it going to be?' And well, here was 'Rascals.' So I said to Ron, 'Take a crack at it because we have to have it.' Ron make it work somehow. But he had gone away hating the project. Ron had been someone from the beginning who just didn't want to have

anything to do with it, but he came back with this wonderful script. He made it so delightful that Rick Berman, the naysayer, called me up and he said, 'I've got to take it back. I'm reading this and it's charming, it's just charming,' and so he was won over and we went ahead with it."

Said Ron Moore who had the unenviable task of writing the show, "I thought it worked better than I thought it was going to. It was not my favorite assignment and it was a difficult show to write."

Rick Berman elaborated, "I was against doing the story too. Michael felt very strongly about it — and I've never gotten in the way of things Michael feels strongly about. To me, the premise was a little bit beyond what I would be willing to swallow. It had a lot of holes in it, some of which we patched up and some of which we just kind of shined on. I think it was a very popular episode, though my level of believability is probably a lot stricter than most of our audience. I think most of our audience would be willing to see us bend the rules more than I might be willing to."

"I had written a quick story last season — the season of the children — and obviously we didn't want to do another child episode," said

Michael Piller. "I felt that there were two very attractive things about the premise. First, was the idea if we could go back to being children again, would we? Is it something we would really enjoy or is it something we would rather forget about? Thematically the idea of doing that would grow as the centerpiece of the show and the relationship between Ro and Guinan. This will sound terribly over-simplified, but there is a very popular, overused reference in psychology these days to discovering the child within you and, in essence, what the show is about is Guinan helping Ro rediscover the child within her. Hopefully the audience sort of enjoyed rediscovering it in themselves and looking at it and finding out what it means. That made it worth doing to me, it made it thematically STAR TREK."

Said Jeri Taylor, "The original premise was that they were really turned into children. There was a lot that would be appealing about that, but what we realized early on was that if they were children with the mental faculties of children, all the adults would do is send them to their room and tell them to go to school while they tried to find a cure, and the story would proceed without them. Because there is no way the children were going to run

around and have any effect on the plot, we realized we needed them to maintain their adult faculties in order for the story to proceed."

"Ever since the story has been around, which is the middle of last season, there's always been a little bit of amazement that we were even considering doing it," said Brannon Braga. "It's insane, but Ron did a great job doing the final rewrite on that episode. It was a really solid script. The problem is you're dealing with kids and they're unpredictable. You're asking them to play adult characters who have been established, who are very good actors. Of course it's going to suffer. All in all, I think its a very good episode. What I objected to are the Ferengi. I think the Ferengi are broad, ill-conceived and ludicrous characters and I hate them. Everytime they appear on the screen with their bad dentures and broad gestures and humor, the show suffers. One might argue they're perfect for 'Rascals' because of the light nature of the material. I feel that they were the absolute wrong choice because it just hurt the credibility of an already preposterous premise."

Jeri Taylor said, "We went through many, many, many different kinds of ideas with that I always had sort of

thought that it might work better if there were a more sinister kind of element to the story pulling against the frivolity of the children. Michael ultimately felt that the Ferengi were going to play more comfortably with the children, because they are somewhat comedic themselves, and it just wouldn't be believable that our children could defeat the Cardassians, for instance, or the Romulans."

"I had a lot of discussions about whether it should be Ferengi because she was afraid that it was so broad an episode already that the Ferengi would only make it broader," said Piller. "I said, 'This is broad, you can't make them the Cardassians or really evil, you gotta play the humor. It has to be a light, fun episode.' I really gave the edict to make them Ferengi and it became THE LITTLE RASCALS for the last half."

Directed by Adam Nimoy, son of actor/director and Vulcan Leonard Nimoy, the lawyer made a decision several years ago to change careers and began studying acting with his father's former acting teacher, Jeff Corey. with the hopes of pursuing a career in directing. "Then I went to work," said Nimoy. "I got a job working as an assistant for Nick Meyer on STAR TREK VI and stuck with him throughout that project. When that project was over, I was looking for something else to do and I called Rick Berman, and he invited me to come on and basically observe, which I did all of last season, unpaid, in all phases of production."

Along with his other training, Nimoy actively sought out the counsel of other STAR TREK directors — including his father — and proceeded to take classes at UCLA as well to hone his skills. "I spent a hell of a lot of time looking at dailies on the set, sitting in on preproduction meetings, going to the post-production process and sitting with the editors. I spent a lot of time with these people hoping to try to convince Rick that I was interested, ambitious and hungry to get onboard."

Spending much of his time with established NEXT GENERATION directors allowed him to get a strong feel for the show. "I had been watching the series, but not that closely," said Nimoy. "There were a few directors that I thought were doing some very interesting work and I stuck to them like glue. Many of them were very nice — nice enough to allow me to hang around and ask questions."

"I thought it was an unfortunate draw for Adam's debut," said actor/director Jonathan Frakes. "He did yeo-

man's work with a story that he didn't have the luxury of having any of the regulars heavy in the show. When a new director comes in, he's often made more comfortable by knowing the show is going to revolve around one of the regulars who knows how to play the part and who knows who the character is. With children, he had restricted hours because of the Screen Actor's Guild rules, and he's dealing with the children's parents who are on the set all the time. It's an unenviable situation. Fortunately, I think he's certainly got a good advisor in his family, far better than I.

For Rick Berman, who's developed a reputation for giving directors their first chance on STAR TREK, Adam Nimoy was no exception. "That was a desperately difficult episode for a first time director to do, and I think Adam did a nice job," said Berman. "He was a lawyer who wanted to learn about film directing and asked if he could come and observe and we said we'd be delighted to have him observe. He started doing what we call 'going to school' and he spent a tremendous amount of time here with no request to direct. After months and months of that he came to me. I decided to give him a crack at something. Unfortunately he was given an episode that would

have been a nightmare for anybody; dealing with four or five kids who were portraying characters that they should have known better than they did and it was a very, very difficult episode."

Commented Nimoy, "I think I was going to be surprised and nervous about whatever came down to me. Everybody assured me that 'Rascals' was a different story, it was an interesting story, therefore it was a challenging story and that it would be a memorable story no matter what I did. That's somewhat helpful. When I think back about STAR TREK episodes from the original series, or even the NEXT GENERATION, I don't necessarily think about who directed them as much as what the story was about. I think that has a lot to do with it. However, I've seen a lot of good directors on this show turn stories that are not that great into something very visually interesting to look at."

Nimoy expressed little concern about his Spock-connection. "There is a lot of nepotism in this business," he noted. "And from my point of view, if I can't deliver the goods, and have no talent, I'm not going to be around for a whole hell of a lot - no matter who my old man is. I think what was helpful was the fact that I had hung around and asked a lot of questions, befriended a lot of people, in an attempt to let them know that I'm not some prima donna who is going to waltz in here and think that I deserve anything. I really did work very, very hard to keep a low profile, but to try to show willingness to be a student and be taken under people's wings, to be taught the ropes, because I am a novice. As a result, I think I had a very good relationship with the crew, in general."

In directing the cast of actors to portray the Enterprise regulars as children, Nimoy found it important to work with their adult counterparts to convey their mannerisms to the youthful dopelgangers. "One of the things I did was to actually talk to Patrick and ask him what were some of the things that he thought he would see in a younger version of himself," said Nimoy. "What were some of his idiosyncrasies and nuances? What type of behavioral things that he would like to see? And we went through the list of what I considered Picard-isms, some of which showed up successfully."

Stewart suggested that Nimoy have David Tristin Birkin [he also played Picard's nephew in "Family"], who essayed the starship captain as a youth, look at several episodes including "The Battle" for an example of his

performance style . "I had David look at them and we watched them together. We went through a whole educational process during the prep to try to get him up to speed to take on some of the characteristics. It was certainly a challenge to be dealing with young kids who were not really experienced actors, because you've got a director who may or may not have some vision, but definitely has no experience. That combination made things a little difficult. However, I thought it was very rewarding. There is always some kind of contingency that you just can't account for as a director and, in this case, I was working with a lot of kids."

Not surprisingly, Nimoy encountered several surprises during the seven-day shoot. "The things that come to mind immediately I think are being on the set and finding out that things are not quite the way they worked out on paper," he said. "When you get there, there are just variables or the camera angles that you didn't see or the things that you can't account for. You have to really be on your toes and be willing to make changes in what you originally planned. An actor might want to do something different than what you had planned and you may feel that their idea really does service the scene and really is better

than what you had in mind. You have to be on your toes to make those changes. I think the biggest responsibility and difficulty that all directors have is to be flexible. You just have to be or you just don't belong there. There are a lot of people who are giving you input and are asking questions and are exploring with you. It is a collaborative process in one shape or another. I think that makes the art better. If you're working with an actor and they have an idea and if it's better than yours, let's make the best thing that we can. Why stick to my piece of paper just because it looked good on paper? I'm happy to accept ideas and make the changes. But then you've got to start working with new camera angles, and where your cuts are going to be, and you're talking to your cinematographer as to whether or not it's going to work. That's the hardest part, when you're there and you're starting from scratch. It's difficult to scrap days and hours of work that you put in of acting moves and camera angles."

Another curve ball for the first-time director are the myriad script changes that can be made on a STAR TREK set during the filming of an episode. "That's common," said Nimoy. "I didn't have it as bad as some directors I've

In "A Fistful of Datas", Data goes the Clint Eastwood route as a gunslinger in a holodeck fantasy gone awry.

seen. It's just another one of those things you've got to be prepared to deal with. There's nothing that you can do about it. It's just the way the game works. I've seen some directors who couldn't prep anything halfway into their prep time because there was no script at all. I've seen that happen again and again. Now some of those guys are very experienced and can deal with that kind of situation. I have to get to speed to where I can do that as well, but I've been for-

tunate enough to have some scripts that are in pretty good shape starting off with my first day of prep."

Following on the heels of "Rascals" was the holodeck romp, "A Fistful Of Datas", which everyone on staff is quick to point out is the first malfunctioning holodeck story to be done in several seasons. "We thought we haven't done this in a while," said Ron Moore. "It used to be cliché, but it's been a few years now, so give it a shot."

The original pitch was made by Robert Hewitt Wolfe, who went on to pitch to DEEP SPACE NINE and was hired as a staff writer on that show. The teleplay was rewritten extensively by Brannon Braga. "This was part of our feeling that we were going to go for more fun ideas," said Michael Piller. "It was an opportunity to let Data and Brent have a field day. Originally it was going to be a story which had Worf getting closer to Troi in a romantic way, but we pulled back on that. When you say Worf and the old west in a shoot out with the android, you're talking about a very wide open, risk taking kind of premise. I thought it was very old STAR TREK and I was trying to recapture a little of the fun that made the old STAR TREK fun to tune into for all age groups. It was successful on that level."

"To think that someone from Great Britain would direct the quintessential American story, which is a western, seems a little oddball, but I think that might have been the happiest thing that happened because Patrick was thrilled at this," said Jeri Taylor of Patrick Stewart's third directorial effort. "He went out and rented every classic western and immersed himself. You could always tell what western Patrick had seen the night before on tape, because he would come in and have a new idea, and it would be a new idea that came from THE MAN WHO KILLED LIBERTY VALANCE or HIGH NOON — and so he just piled all of it in there and it just worked gloriously. It was a tough production, we had to go on location and he had a lot to do out there. It just had a smashing look and it was just tons of fun."

"Patrick did a wonderful job directing, which I think is hilarious," echoed Naren Shankar. "The funniest thing is

Brannon doesn't know anything about westerns either so he was writing a western directed by an Englishman."

"I've seen very few westerns; THE SEARCHERS, ONE EYED JACKS, UNFORGIVEN," said Braga. "It was ironic that I was handed this not being familiar with the western genre, and Patrick Stewart, who was even less familiar, was going to direct it. It brought a freshness to it and I think this show was more fun to write than any other. I really enjoyed doing it. The first draft, which was written by Robert Wolfe, didn't have a solid western story and it needed one, so I watched RIO BRAVO and that's the story I decided to kind of utilize for the holodeck fantasy. They're obviously different. I became a lover of the western genre and watched dozens of them and my favorite was THE OUTLAW JOSIE WALES and THE SEARCHERS. What great movies. I must have watched 25 westerns and those three were superior."

In the original Wolfe story, Alexander's plan was to bring Troi and Worf together romantically. The subplot was quickly deleted. "It was an intriguing notion," said Jeri Taylor. "It just seemed less interesting than other things that were going on. It seemed like more of a soap opera sort

of thing. That's the kind of story that you can see on the air anywhere. Every sitcom has children with separated, divorced parents, and all that kind of thing. It's not an element on STAR TREK I want to concentrate on much more. I think we probably just mined out all the stories about Alexander and Worf's problems as a daddy. It was beginning to feel very much like contemporary family drama, and we really made an effort to break Worf out of that and give him back his Klingon-hood, rather than to make him a suburban, single father, which is how a lot of that was feeling."

"I cut the Troi and Alexander story right away because it felt false to me," said Brannon Braga. "This was a holodeck romp and it should be light and fun. Then I pumped up the Data acting bizarre angle a little bit. It was a lot of fun and satisfying to come up with a good gag for the end. What was going to be special about this gunfight? What was going to make it STAR TREK? Suddenly, that's where it needed to be STAR TREK again, when you have Worf defeating the holodeck villain in a special STAR TREK way. I thought the force field was fun as were the characters' reactions to it. The one thing I miss was that in my draft there was a Data as a bandito scene with an Alexander scene that was inspired by 'Ransom of Red Chief', where basically you have the bandito holding Alexander hostage in the cave."

The character of Alexander has stirred mixed feelings not only among fans, but on the staff as well, where he has proved to be to be an unwanted addition to some since coming aboard the ship in last year's episode "New Ground."

"Part of the problem we've had is that the actor has not been available to us," said Jeri Taylor of the former FAMILY TIES actor Brian Bonsall. "He was off doing a feature. We had a story that I still consider a very powerful story, that would have done something very interesting with Alexander and solved all of our problems. Michael absolutely despised the story. My one disappointment from this year is my not being able to do that story, and I kept trying and I kept writing it up in different ways and giving it to him, and he finally said, 'Don't give this to me anymore.' In my heart of hearts, I still would like to see that story develop, and it would take care of our problems."

"There is a risk in the sixth season of becoming bored with characters you've

been writing for six years," said Michael Piller. "Occasionally out of the staff would come a crazy idea like, 'We don't feel the Alexander character is working, let's send him off to a strange planet where he becomes a teenager, loses his youth and goes off to fight a war' or something like that. I would say no, that character doesn't have to go away because you don't feel like writing him. If you don't have anything new to say about him right now, move on and he can be down going to school somewhere. He doesn't have to be in every episode that Worf is in."

Explained Brannon Braga, "We frequently must ignore Alexander because we don't want to put him in the episode. We'd rather not use a half a page explaining him."

Despite being one of the show's most humorous and light-hearted episodes, Jeri Taylor has reservations about the production. "The one thing I wasn't happy about is that everybody was drinking and smoking in 'Fistful of Datas.' I don't like that and when our regulars are seen smoking — and I'm sure this was Patrick's choice and it is true to the genre, but Troi smoking, Data smoking and tossing back shots, which is a western motif, made me uncomfortable. I felt we were sending the message, especially to our

young people, that our heroes consider that sort of an acceptable thing to do."

In "Quality of Life," Data must confront a decision as to whether he should violate orders and risk Picard's life to preserve what he considers a new life form. "This was a story that I sort of read and said, 'I don't know, we've done that, haven't we?'" recalled Jeri Taylor. "It was a story that Michael really liked, and so I said 'Fine, we need any story we can get going.' The task then became how to tell it in a way that didn't make it a repeat of things we have seen before, which include the Nannites in 'Evolution' and Data in 'Measure of a Man'. By having it be a Data story, it sort of took it away from 'Measure of a Man', because it's Data himself standing up for these beings. It was Naren Shankar's first full script for us, before he was on staff, and it was the script that made me realize that he deserved his chance to prove himself, because he really did a very thoughtful, thorough, sensitive job with it."

"I thought everything about it was very nice except the doctor's costume," said Rene Echevarria. "She looked like the gingerbread lady. Not giving it away was the challenge. It would have been very easy to make it very clear they were a life form and the danger was the audience would be with Data from the first minute and thinking how horrible of Captain Picard and everybody else not to believe him. That line was very difficult to walk. I think Naren did a pretty good job with that. It didn't go too far in the anthropormorisation of them."

Making an encore appearance in "Ship in a Bottle" was Professor Moriarty, who had first appeared in second season's "Elementary, Dear Data." The Holmes-ian mythos had been noticeably absent from the final frontier due to a disagreement with the Arthur Conan Doyle estate stemming from the studio's use of the characters in YOUNG SHERLOCK HOLMES. When the staff checked into usage again this year, they found that the Holmes estate would gladly license use of the characters for a nominal fee. "I've always loved any efforts Brent has had to play the Sherlock Holmes character, and the two instances where he has put on a Holmesian quality has been wonderful," said Rick Berman. "The character of Daniel Davis frozen in our computer memory waiting to be brought back to life someday was something I couldn't imagine we wouldn't want to get back to eventually. It was a charming episode which I really

liked a lot."

"For years we'd been told, you can't do it," said Jeri Taylor. "Paramount said no after YOUNG SHERLOCK HOLMES had gotten into a fight with the Holmes estate and they said never again. And so we said, 'Oh, okay. Never again. Too bad, that was a great thing.' I opened this inquiry again, though, and we set something in motion that was the beginning when I called our legal person and she called back and said, 'Oh, that's very easy. It's X number of dollars,' which wasn't very much, 'and you can have Moriarty.' I said, 'You're kidding me.' And she said, 'No, no. They've done this for someone else here and they're very happy.' Everyone was astonished and Brent was thrilled and amazed because he'd been told he could never do it again."

Barclay, who had returned in "Realm of Fear" after having appeared in third and fourth season episodes, returned in "Ship In A Bottle." "There was something intriguing about the notion of Moriarty, the most evil man in the universe seducing poor Barclay," said Ron Moore. "You know, it was just the most naive and kind of neurotic guy to introduce. That seemed like a good combination."

"Aquiel" satisfied anoth-

er long held desire on the part of the writing staff, which was to involve Chief Engineer Geordi La Forge in a real romantic relationship. Even the actor had admitted to growing tired of his obsessions with imaginary holodeck recreations and rebuffs from "platonic" friends. "Michael said he had seen a film called LAURA and thought we could do a love story for Geordi based on LAURA," explained Rene Echevarria of the show's high-concept origins in the classic film noir with Gene Tierney and Dana Andrews. "Basically, somebody falls in love with a dead person and then they show up. That was the genesis of it. The best stories obviously come from an idea you have, so this was kind of working backwards."

Said Michael Piller. "LAURA was one prototype I threw out. It felt like it was sort of related in a way since we had shown Geordi falling in love with holodeck figures, so why not take it one step removed and show him falling in love with the picture of the dead woman and then finding out that she's still alive?"

STAR TREK rarely uses other films as a catalyst for energizing the creative juices as many television shows do, seizing on a prototype and making it their own. Such films as SILENCE OF THE LAMBS

David Warner, who had roles as a human diplomat in Star Trek V: The Final Frontier *and the Klingon Chancellor in* Star Trek VI: The Undiscovered Country, *became a Caradassian torturer in "Chain of Command". Here he is seen as Jack the Ripper in* Time After Time *(photo copyright © 1979 Warner Bros.)*

had become a joke in pitch meetings as writer after writer came in after that film opened, taunting stories in which Troi encounters brilliant, psychotic being ferried aboard the Enterprise. However, even STAR TREK isn't above occasionally having an idea sparked by the silver screen as was again the case with Naren Shankar's teleplay for "Face of The Enemy."

Said Rene Echevarria of the story which takes place primarily aboard a Romulan warbird, "At some point I was free and we had this notion of doing THE HUNT FOR RED OCTOBER with Troi as a Romulan. It

was sort of a staff premise. It was basically two sets; her room and the bridge and you can afford to do two acts before you start to feel claustrophobic. As a result, structurally it was a perfect thing to be able to jump to the Enterprise after that. I thought it had a good pace and a good story for Troi and a couple of twists. It was a very conscious effort to give her something commanding, with tough choices to be made. Apparently it was very popular."

Season Six also included two mid-season two part episodes, both of which marked dramatic departures in traditional storytelling for the

show. "I've never been against doing a two parter if it was a story that called for it," said Rick Berman. "Often we've had stories that are one-parters that writers would love to expand into two parts. One of the problems we had this year was that 'Chain of Command' would have aired three weeks apart when we looked down at our rerun schedule because there were two repeats stuck in the middle. I had to deal with Paramount in kind of reworking airdate schedules to make that work, which we managed to successfully do."

"Chain of Command" became a two-parter when

• • • •

Original model designed to be used as the Klingon/Romulan compound in "Birthright"

Michael Piller latched onto the storyline in which Picard is tortured by a Cardassian. While the idea was hard to resist, so was the notion of being able to save money on what would virtually amount to two characters in a room. The second two part episode was "Birthright", which was cleaved for similar reasons.

"It started out as a one-parter about the idea of Worf finding these Klingons who didn't want to admit they were alive and who wouldn't leave their prison," said Jeri Taylor. "We broke the whole story and thought this is a really good story, Michael's going to love this. Because we're always a little apprehensive when he comes in and sits down, we start running it through and eyeing him to see if he likes it. His brow furrows and you think, 'Oh no, he doesn't like this, we're going to have to do it over again.' So that day he sat there and his brow got one furrow and then it got two and then it got seven. Somewhere near the end he started looking out the window like he had just dismissed even thinking about it. It was so wretched. And I was just in anguish. This is a wonderful story. Have we missed the boat? What is going on?' Michael just seemed to loath it. And so Ron finished and we turned around and looked at Michael. He didn't say anything for a long time. Obviously, he was thinking and thinking and thinking. It seemed like an eternity before he spoke, and then he said, 'Okay, it can't work, it can't work.' I thought he meant it can work but it needs a complete restructure. And he said, 'This is just too good. This is too good not to do a two-parter.....I think, you know, you're rushing the story. You're trying to cram too much in. I think it just has to be a two-parter.' So all of our interpretations — which were he hates this and we're going to have to do it over — was really this was so good that we can't rush it.

Once it was determined the storyline would be

expanded into two parts, the challenge then became finding a B-story for the first part, which surprisingly materialized as one of the highlights of the season.

"We had the formidable task of stretching it out and figuring out what amounted to another episode," said Taylor. "And the whole Data thing started in desperation and just saying, 'What can we do with Data? What haven't we done with Data?' So from the Klingons sort of having a mystical, mythical, spiritual side, we thought, well, maybe Data can be exploring a metaphysical aspect or a spiritual side to himself. Does he have this? He keeps trying to get it and doesn't. And that just kept getting turned and turned until almost at the last minute it became the dreaming thing, which Brannon then took and made this magical, wonderful, literally soaring kind of B story that rightly took over the first part. The first part of two is usually just sort of getting to the provocative ending, and often you're sort of tap dancing through it. But he turned it into magic. To me, that whole story by itself is one of the best we've ever done."

Said Brannon Braga, "The nice thing about 'Birthright I' was that you have a closure in the Data story, which I think some people

expected to go on in Part Two. Then the second story moved off, which is nice to have in a two-parter. It was a unique structure we had never tried before, it worked quite well and we may try it again. We'll do it if we need to. It just happened that way. I can see us doing a three-parter if the story warrants it."

From the philosophically challenging "Birthright" duo, the writers segued into a pure action/adventure or "run and jump," as such shows are referred to on STAR TREK. In "Starship Mine," Picard inadvertently stumbles onto a plot to steal trilithium from the ship's engines by criminals after the Enterprise has been evacuated for a routine baryon sweep.

While the writers have traditionally expressed an aversion to non-character driven action, "Starship Mine" proved an important vehicle for Patrick Stewart, an actor whose continuing happiness has proven foremost on the producers' minds. As his stature has grown on the show over the years, so has his clout, as is standard for a lead actor on a hit television series.

"Morgan Gendel came in with 'Starship Mine' and I knew it was a strange kind of premise for STAR TREK, but we really hadn't serviced Patrick well in the beginning of the

year and I think Patrick was beginning to feel that," said Jeri Taylor. "There were a lot of episodes that didn't really focus on him and when you have someone like Patrick, that's not a good idea. It's off-beat and unusual for us and I thought it was just a hoot. What we look for are fascinating, interesting stories, and that's everybody's first standard. I am not an action adventure fan and so I wouldn't want to do a season on 'Starship Mine,' but I said 'Hey, great idea, Picard running around like an action hero.' I think that's different, that's unexpected, that's unusual. It doesn't represent my kind of feeling about the kinds of things that I would ordinarily like to develop. I think that's probably true of a lot of people, but it seemed like a really good, entertaining idea."

"That's what's great about this season," added Brannon Braga. "You do something like 'Birthright' and then you leap into pure action. There's also more humor and action in that episode than perhaps we've done the whole season, except in 'A Fistful of Datas.'"

"We joke it's about command," laughed Rene Echevarria, attempting to explain how 'Starship Mine' can be considered metaphorical, as he is reluctant to admit that STAR TREK would deviate from character-driven drama. "The rest is run and jump on the ship, Picard outwitting the terrorists. There's not a big character arc. The idea is basically DIE HARD and the scenes with Data are hilarious."

It soon became apparent that the well was beginning to run dry again after "Starship Mine", and the staff once more scrambled to resuscitate ideas that could be considered producible. "The Chase" was a story that had first been discussed on the same trip to Michael Piller's vacation home in Mexico last year that gave birth to "I, Borg", "The Perfect Mate", and "First Duty".

"It was begun then and languished because once it was written, Michael wasn't real fond of it," said Jeri Taylor of the story in which bitter enemies find out they share much in common. "He thought it had real problems and Rick despised it. He felt, and rightly so, in that incarnation that it was cartoonish and silly. There were all these roadblocks and once again we got dry and we said what do we have, and there was 'The Chase'. We just went ahead and broke the story, which was a very daring and scary thing to do."

Joe Menosky, a former NEXT GENERATION Executive

The enormously popular Bruce Willis film **Die Hard** very obviously served as the inspiration for "Starship Mine" in which Picard takes on a team of terrorists who have boarded a near-vacant Enterprise (photo copyright © 1988 20th Century Fox).

Script Consultant, who had taken a European sabbatical from writing and had first conceived of the script concept, worked with Ron Moore in breaking it.

"We gave it to him because it was his and Ron's idea originally, and they broke it in a day. Then they brought in Michael, who we knew had to be won over — which was

not a situation you want to be in," said Taylor. "He loved it and said, 'It's wonderful and if we could save it to be the last episode, that's what we should do. It's such a Roddenberry-esque message, it's so humanistic in what it has to say, that if there's any way you could not do it here and do it at the end of the season, then do that.' I said, 'I can't, that's why we went ahead and did this because we don't have anything else.'"

Said Rene Echevarria, "The idea is that we find out the reason why everyone in the galaxy that we deal with is a biped with something on their forehead. An ancient race has seeded the galaxy with their genes and left a piece of code in the genes that if everyone got together, they would get the message and learn the truth. It's this wonderful moment where everyone thinks it's a weapon or it's this or that, and this creature appears in a holograph and says 'You're all brothers and sisters'. As soon as it's over, the moment is shattered and it's this great irony that the creature says 'If you're here it must be that you came together in brotherhood.' It's a lovely moment and a nice explanation for something that probably troubles a lot of people."

"'The Chase' to me is classic STAR TREK," noted Brannon Braga. "It signaled Joe Menosky's return to STAR TREK. It was delightful and I think it will certainly be a classic TREK episode. The message of this show will be remembered more than any other episode this season, maybe more than any other message of any episode of all time."

As the season continued, the dearth of workable concepts once again presented itself. As late as March, the last several episodes remained elusive. "We were desperate," admitted Jeri Taylor. "We were getting more and more behind, which you do all the time because the season catches up with you. The juggernaut is rolling downhill and coming at you faster. We had less and less lead time, and the guys were spread thin. Brannon said, 'What about Riker in an insane asylum?' and with about that much of a premise, we wrote three sentences and gave it to Rick and Michael and they said, 'There's nothing here, it's not even a premise — it's a starting point and this is real cliched and everybody does an insane asylum story.' I don't know if they do, but with that sort of disdainful response we once again went ahead and started breaking it. We didn't have a story, didn't know what it was going to be, no one had seen a story, but we had to move on it and we went upstairs to Ron's office and hammered it out. The arguments about that story got as heated as it ever has and I thought, 'Are we ever going to get this done? Are we going to die here? Are we going to shut down production? Am I going to be responsible for the first time production has ever had to shut down on STAR TREK?"

The result was "Frame of Mind", Brannon Braga's challenging, dark and disturbing vehicle for Riker in which he believes he has gone insane. "Through that conflictual dissenting kind of debate we came onto a concept which was far from the original idea and so unique and captivating we would have never gotten to it in any other way," said Taylor. "It got down and Michael and he came upstairs, having already announced he had a lot of trouble with this and didn't expect much. We went through it and he said 'Write it, it's incredible what you've done.' Without that process of breaking the story where people can hammer it out, you don't necessarily get to those levels. It really keeps you off balance and Jonathan is phenomenal in it."

Said Rick Berman, "This was a script that I liked fro. day one. It was quite different. I'm not a big fan of fooling the audience and I've always tried to avoid stories that fooled the audience. On the other hand, this did it in a way that I found acceptable. I think it had a lot of wonderful twists and turns in it and I think Jonathan did a great job. I've never been a big fan of the episodes that proceed, proceed, proceed, proceed and in the last scene you're told exactly what's happened. It's kind of like the sci-

• • • •

ence-fiction version of COLUMBO, where the great detective at the end tells everybody what they've been watching and there's a little of that here, but for people who are crazy enough to go back and look at these things a second time, I think there's wonderful little foreshadowings and clues. It's a very enigmatic episode that I got a kick out of."

In an effort to end the year, another tried and true concept was turned on its head: that of the murder/mystery, in which a Ferengi is murdered onboard the Enterprise, prompting Dr. Crusher to lead an investigation that has her come into conflict with Picard over it. The story can trace its genesis back to a far different storyline which had existed for some time, but gone unrealized. "It was a difficult show and had a very tortured history," said Naren Shankar. "The show started as an episode Joe Menosky wrote at the end of the fifth season called 'Limits', and this investigation of an anomaly and a murder with lots of scientists onboard — a Romulan and a Klingon — and that went through a couple of drafts. The show was put on hold until we revived it this year as a Beverly murder mystery. The idea of Beverly as Quincy is kind of an interesting premise and it just became a very difficult show going

Dr. Crusher (Gates McFadden) puts her career on the line as she investigates the death of a Ferengi scientist in "Suspicions" (photo copyright © 1993 Karen Witkowski).

through a lot of rewrites. It's very hard to get mystery right."

Originally, "Limits", which had also briefly been considered for the season cliffhanger, featured a scientific puzzle that intrigued Shankar into wanting to write the episode. To his chagrin, the scientific dilemma was dropped, leaving him with a murder for Beverly to solve, a far cry from Menosky's original idea. "The premise of 'Limits' was that warp drive itself was weakening the fabric of space and time," said Shankar. "It was sort of a pollution show and that by traveling through space we're causing these problems. The idea at the end was that there would have to

be certain areas of the galaxy that were restricted for low-warp travel. It's an interesting idea and it could have been a nice ecological show about all different races needing to work together. That's what I wanted — and what I ended up with was a show with that premise being taken out of it and the idea of this murder mystery with Beverly. We had to break it three times before Michael bought it and even then it didn't quite go as well as we hoped. I was a little bit intimidated by it because I don't feel so confident writing a murder mystery. It's not a genre I particularly care for and it becomes very plot heavy."

"We called it the

'Limits' curse," said Brannon Braga. "Naren showed some interest in the environmental angle and the environmental angle was promptly dropped. He was stuck with the mystery and someone had the brilliant script notion of making Dr. Crusher Quincy, which was a really good idea. Sometimes we joke that 'Limits' was the show that broke Joe — after two drafts he was just so tired he left the show. I think we broke 'Suspicions' three times and each time Mike threw it out. Finally, we had it and the script was turned in and he hated it."

"'Suspicions" is off-concept in that it is relayed as a series of voice-over flashbacks by Dr. Crusher in the style of classic film noir, ala D.O.A. or DOUBLE INDEMNITY. "Those are things we had to ask permission to do," said Jeri Taylor. "It is a very stylistically different show. It's a Beverly story in which she solves a murder mystery and so she sort of has a Sam Spade kind of voice-over and we've never done that. We've never done flashbacks, we've never done voice-overs. All we've done is the logs, and there was some feeling that we never would, but we felt if you do it once, it's not establishing a trend. It's simply breaking tradition and that can be refreshing."

"Suspicions" prompted

Michael Piller's most active involvement of the season. As a life-long mystery buff, Piller tackled the rewrite of the show to conform to his expectations for the piece. "This was a tough show and this was the one show I got heavily involved in," said Piller. "I just didn't think it was working well into pre-production and we basically tore it apart and put it back together again, and changed the whole nature of the mystery and some other substantial changes. The script is much, much better than it was three days before the start of shooting. It was a show that was being written during the first few days of production."

After "Suspicions", Ron Moore returned to familiar turf with "Rightful Heir", in which Worf re-examines his Klingon heritage. "It's quite a spiritual show and an interesting examination of gods and renewal," said Michael Piller. "I think you have to really be into Klingons to enjoy it, but if you are, you're going to love it and it's a very thoughtful, provocative and well written script. I think that the universe of STAR TREK has room for all philosophies. I think that's fundamental in Gene's vision. There was an edit done in the last draft of something Ron wanted to do — that I doubted and Rick hated — which was Worf really does have a vision, he really does see

K'ehlst and that might have been too far, by making God suddenly exist on the Enterprise. But in terms of belief and the structure of a STAR TREK dealing with spirituality, I feel there's absolutely room for it and doesn't go against anything Gene established."

Said Jeri Taylor of "Rightful Heir's" debt to "Birthright", "I think it was getting into the whole cultural identity and Worf wanting to touch more of what his roots are and seeing the impact that it had on the young people. I think it brings him very organically to an acknowledgment of what we are calling a spiritual crisis or spiritual lack. With the Klingons we can explore a realm we couldn't explore with our humans. Although I personally am completely atheistic, I think that it's very nice for us to suggest there's a spirituality in the 24th century. To many people that's an important part of their lives and I don't deny that or denigrate it at all. I think that it's not right to have it antiseptically stripped from the future. Here is a chance to acknowledge those kinds of needs in people and the importance that spirituality has to fill those needs. It offers a sense of comfort and tradition and ritual and cultural identity for people, and we found a nifty sci-fi way of doing it."

Noted Rick Berman, "I had a lot of fights with Ron about this. The character of K'lest, the backstory, the dialogue of K'lest were all a little bit too on the nose Christ-like for me. We had a lot of long debates on this and eventually it was modified by Ron in a way that I think made it much better. I think he not only solved my problems but made the show better. Kevin Conway's performance is great and it's a wonderful episode."

The season concluded with a spectacular cliffhanger in which the Borg and Lore returned to menace the Enterprise. "We heard lots of Borg pitches," said Naren Shankar. "We finally came up with a direction to take them in after 'I, Borg.' There was one other story we had developed and spent sometime developing which would have been fun. This story was about the Enterprise being decommissioned, but there were a number of problems with it. Rick and Mike never bought into it and then the Borg story came along and we started talking about it."

"We struggled long and hard to decide if we wanted to do a cliffhanger. I felt if we did a lousy cliffhanger it would put a bad feeling on the season," said Michael Piller. "I did not want to force ourselves to do a cliffhanger if it didn't work. It

has become something of a tradition, but I didn't want to do it if it wasn't a good story. I killed two or three of them and Jeri came up with 'Descent', which was not a Borg show to begin with. It was a show that had to deal with an invasion of space creatures and they turned out to be working for Lore. I wanted to do it as a cliffhanger involving DEEP SPACE NINE, a crossover, but Rick did not want to do that so we left it to the NEXT GENERATION. Now, there was still a concern that there was not really an inherent interest in a new set of space monsters, so they came up with an idea that had been tossed around since we did 'I, Borg': what happens when Hugh goes back and chats with the other Borg? I *am* a little concerned that it's another Borg cliffhanger and that by its very nature it will be compared to the first Borg cliffhanger. But it only has to be effective to be successful, it doesn't need to top 'Best of Both Worlds.'"

"We've completely upended them [the Borg] and turned them into fanatics," said Jeri Taylor. "They will look like Borg but they won't walk, talk or quack like Borg at all. I think there's enough of a radical change having Lore as the menace who commandeered them and turned them into fighting machines and Lore's

ethnic cleansing, if you will. That's the tact we're taking on it. Ultimately, the brothers having to deal with each other in that sort of mythic slaying of the evil brother."

Even as Ron Moore finished worked on the finale, Rene Echevarria began working on the resolution of the cliffhanger for next season. "For once we're doing it my way," said Taylor. "We have a story that hasn't been approved, but at least we have an idea where we're going for a change which we've never done before."

As the staff prepares for the next season, they will have less time than usual to gear up for the final year of the show. Because the NEXT GENERATION feature film will begin shooting in April, the summer hiatus has been cut by about a month and as a result the writing staff will have even less time than usual to prepare for the last twenty-six episodes of the show's seven year run. Fortunately, several ideas are already in the works.

"We have set some character things in place we'd like to explore," said Brannon Braga. "Data's dreaming, Geordi has a romance he's initiated and there are some other things that were happening towards the end of the season that we can go back to. Certainly, I would like to see

The worlds of both Next Generation and Deep Space were recently covered in the pages of Cinefantastique.

the high concepts continue where each show is really different and exciting. We're in an arena in the last season of a show where you can tell almost any kind of story, which is different than any other show in history in some ways, except maybe for the TWILIGHT ZONE We're always looking for ways to tell totally unique stories that can't be told on any other venue. We've all got the feeling we want to make it very special."

Offered Naren Shankar, "People always ask, 'Where do you get the ideas for the shows?' It's been on for six years and we still don't have a real shortage of ideas. I think that speaks very well of the staff and the people who come in to pitch to us, as well as the interest in the show. The thing about STAR TREK is you can keep going with it. Seven years doesn't have to be the end of the show. If everyone wants to keep doing it, we can keep going. It's my first job in Hollywood and I'm delighted to be on the staff of a number one show, and I don't think anyone would disagree with me. It's had the rare good fortune to have the right mixture of talent and people and in six years it's gone on an upwards trajectory getting better. There are not many shows that can say that and it's a real tribute to Rick, Michael, Jeri, Ron,

Brannon and everybody else who have been on the show for the last few years."

"As far as the show is concerned, I would like it to be the best year we've ever had," said Brent Spiner. "I think everyone hopes for that in its final season, but I don't know what would make it the best year because it's been a very strong show for *six* years."

For fans who expect closure in the show's final season, they are bound to be disappointed. As Jeri Taylor pointed out, the staff has no intention of providing a bookend for the small screen missions of the Starship Enterprise.

"We're already saying this is the last cliffhanger we will have," said Taylor. "I don't know that we're going to wrap it up. I don't think that's ever happened in the series. We don't wrap things up. Jack Crusher is an example of that. Besides which, there are going to be features. So their lives don't come to an end and you leave the story continuing. I think that it probably will be a nicer season if we let it happen as it happens, as we always have, rather than trying to mold it and shape it into something just because we think it's going to be the last season. That just feels too manipulative. It's worked very well just being organic and I see no reason why this season

can't be the same. One reason my anxiety level has diminished is because I'm not in a desperate hunt for writers. I know I have people who can do it, they all know the show and we've lived through a lot together. It's a well-oiled machine and there is a lot to be said for that. Chaos is not good for anyone."

Nonetheless, the staff, some of who have been working on the series for as long as four years, express a degree of sadness over the fact that they are entering what will probably be their final year toiling in the 24th century.

"I'm a huge fan of NEXT GENERATION," said Brannon Braga. "I did not watch the show, I tried a few episodes the first season and for whatever reason it wasn't engaging. I've never seen the original series but I'm a huge fan of this show at this point, having written on the show for three years, and no more was that more painfully evident to me than when a rumor was going around a few months ago that there wouldn't be a seventh season. We were all in the dark and I was very depressed. I really felt this show deserved a seventh season. I just now feel we're breaking it open in writing terms. As a writer, I felt the show is extremely ambitious and is growing. It could go on for ten years. Why cut it off at six? I was very depressed at the prospect of losing NEXT GENERATION."

"I hope STAR TREK is always around in some incarnation," he continued. "It's a great concept. This core writing staff has been in place for three years. We've all grown together and we practically read each other's minds and function as one mind. In a way, we've become a STAR TREK concept, the collective mind, and now we're exploring new facets of our consciousness. Hopefully it will come to some dramatic fruition next season. In terms of the seventh season, it's a mixture of melancholy, apprehension and excitement. I'm sad that it may be the last season and I'm apprehensive because we've got 26 shows to fill.

None of us know what this season will be like. I think one goal we all have is to push the limits of the show once again and make it the best season yet."

••••

EPISODE GUIDE
Season Six

"Times Arrow, Part II"

"Man of the People"

"Relics"

"Schisms"

"True Q"

"Rascals"

"A Fistful of Datas"

"The Quality of Life"

" Chain of Command, Part I"

"Chain of Command, Part II"

"Ship in a Bottle"

"Aquiel"

"Face of the Enemy"

"Tapestry"

"Birthright, Part I"

"Birthright, Part II"

"Starship Mine"

"Lessons"

"The Chase"

"Frame of Mind"

"Suspicions"

"Rightful Heir"

"Second Chances"

"Timescape"

"Descent"

The Episodes

Episode #127
"Times Arrow, Part II"

Teleplay by Jeri Taylor
Story by Joe Menosky
Directed by Les Landau

Guest Starring:
Whoopi Goldberg (Guinan), Jerry Hardin (Samuel Clemens), Alexander Enberg (Young Reporter), Van Epperson (Morgue Attendant), Pamela Kosh (Mrs. Carmichael), Michael Aron (Jack the Bellboy), James Gleason (Dr. Appollinaire), Bill Cho Lee (Male Patient), William Boyett (Policeman), Mary Stein (Alien Nurse)

The Away Team enters the temporal distortion on Devida Two and finds itself in the 19th century, hoping to rescue Data and put an end to the murders on Earth by strange alien life forms who have been traveling back in time to feed on human neural energy. While the Away Team attempts to return to the 24th century, Samuel Clemens (Jerry Hardin) is inadvertently transported to the future, where he is brought aboard the Enterprise, while Picard remains trapped back in time with Guinan and Data's head.

"There is still a whole middle part of their relationship that's missing and may forever be missing," said Jeri Taylor of Guinan and Picard's enigmatic friendship. "This is not a series where we feel we have to explain everything about everybody. Jack Crusher's death has never been explained and may never be. What happened to Picard and Guinan when they met again may never be either, but the idea that they had met in the past 300 years ago just seemed too provocative an idea to ignore."

Taylor's only sole teleplay credit of the season avoided much of the heavy science-fiction elements set forth in the fifth season cliffhanger.

"I felt the first episode got mired in technobabble," she said. "We wanted to try to stay away from that. I think that in a sense, we might have gone too far, because I'm not sure that a lot of it was ever explained. I think it might still be mystifying to people just what were those aliens up to and why they were doing it. Everytime we started to get into all this long stuff again, we decided we'd just go with the fun."

Laughed Brannon Braga of the show's impenetrable time travel scenario, "Breaking 'Time's Arrow II' was a fascinating and almost impossible process. Jeri Taylor went through hell writing that script because it was so complicated. In Part One not only weren't a lot of people sure what the answers were, a lot of people weren't even sure what the questions were. There was a whole B plot about the aliens and what they were trying to do and who they were, which had to be dropped because there just wasn't enough room in people's brains to assimilate it."

"I thought some of the science was a little intangible in Part One," said Ron Moore. "Part Two is a little more fun in terms of seeing our actors in those costumes and Riker hitting the policeman. I don't think I was satisfied with the Mark Twain part. I felt that we didn't give him his due. To take that sort of historical figure and put him on the starship for an episode felt like there should be more than just one walk through the corridor with Troi. Unfortunately, there was so much story to tell that the needs of the show forced you into really moving that into a sidebar and just playing a scene here and there."

"That was my first episode on staff and we broke it together and it was very tough," recalled Rene Echevarria. "We basically boxed ourselves into a corner with Part One and it prompted very hilarious arguments about time travel and how it worked. 'That's not how time travel works, you idiot', with huge accusations and people falling

The readers of Starlog recently chose the 25 best episodes of Next Generation, among them sixth season's "Relics" and "A Fistful of Datas" (cover copyright © 1993 Starlog Communications International).

For "Time's Arrow", Star Trek *make-up magician Michael Westmore created a duplicate of Data's head (photo courtesy David Ian Salter)*

back on primary sources like BILL & TED'S EXCELLENT ADVENTURE. 'That's the way it works, you can so meet yourself!' and all sorts of preposterous stuff."

Scenes of Data in Part One had been shot on soundstages and on location at Pico House in Downtown Los Angeles. The more expansive visualization of the past era became a point of contention when the studio tried to convince the production team to use their new $10 million New

York Street instead of shooting turn-of-the century San Francisco at Universal.

"We were all ready to shoot at Universal, and we had a meeting with the studio who was concerned that we were not fairly evaluating the New York Street that they had built," recalled David Livingston. "They wanted to make it clear to us that the New York street was there. I knew it was there, I walk by it every day. I had a twinge of conscious when I left the meeting because I had put

a strong case for the fact that we had looked at the New York street, evaluated it and decided that it was not appropriate for the show and that Universal was much better. And as I was leaving the meeting, I said, 'Wait a minute, David, are you being totally fair?' I'm a company man, but I am also interested in putting the most money on the screen and getting the most bang for the buck. I asked myself if we were really making the right decision, going over to another

• • • •

studio and paying for all it costs to go over there, spending a lot of money for renting a facility when we might make better use of our facilities. So, I asked that the production designer and the director reevaluate the lot here, and try and make it work. And they did, and I thought the results were wonderful."

Differed Production Designer Richard James, "I didn't feel that New York street at Paramount was the proper scale for us in San Francisco because of Part I, where we had used that downtown location which I felt was more like the scale of San Francisco, especially for that period where San Francisco was much smaller. I felt that it was kind of a stretch to make it look like we had used the same city for Part I and Part II. The Universal location that we had selected was really good. It was right on and picked up even some details from the other location in Part I that we had and some of the brick that was there. I felt much more comfortable with it."

Ultimately, James was convinced that the Paramount street could work, pointing out that "the dollar rising its ugly head" was one of their most important con-siderations. Working with new NEXT GENERATION Director of Photography Jonathan West and director Les Landau, they assessed the set and realized that the look of the backlot was not the only problem they faced.

"It has no ends," said James. "We had a chase and there's no way for the camera to turn and watch because that set is designed so you can't turn the camera and look down a street and get both sides of the street at the same time because you see Stage 32 down the street. There's no way to really shoot it from that angle. What we did is we found shots that if we hugged one side of the building in our right frame line we could get across the street, get that turn in and avoid all the open space. So we did kind of cheat things like that."

"I think the way that Les directed it and the way the extras were used and the use of long lenses, and some of the art direction that we did, worked," said David Livingston. "One of the reasons we didn't use it originally was because there were a lot of metal fire escapes and stuff which were not in San Francisco during that time period, but we had them removed and you can't even tell where it was shot."

Added James, "When it was all said and done, the story is visually strong and the interiors of the boarding house and the morgue and the infirmary, which we built on set, have a lot going for us. People looked great in their costumes and hair and make-up and it's fun to see our people in that kind of a setting."

For Marina Sirtis, who was packed into a corset for the episode, the period shoot was playtime. "It was fun," she said. "I spent most of my career in period costume in England, but, of course, it's never that hot there so you're never that uncomfortable. It was nice to use the corsets, things that we were so uncomfortable in, since I would imagine someone coming back in time from the 24th century would be. It's always playtime when we have to do those things. Robin Hood ['Q-Pid'] was playtime and those are the real fun episodes where we just let loose. It's like kindergarten on the set. We had a director in the first season who has refused to come back because we were too rowdy and that was in the first season. We're *much* rowdier now, so we definitely won't be seeing him again."

Dwight Schultz, seen here with Mr. T on The A-Team, *has become something of a recurring character on* Next Generation *as Barclay (photo copyright © 1982 MCA).*

Episode #128
"Realm of Fear"

**Written by Brannon Braga
Directed by Cliff Bole**

Guest Starring:
Dwight Schultz (Reginald Barclay), Colm Meaney (O'Brien), Renata Scott (Admiral Hayes), Thomas Velgrey (Crew Member), Patti Yasutake (Nurse Ogawa), Majel Barrett (Computer Voice)

Resident Enterprise milquetoast Barclay (Dwight Schultz) is attacked by a strange creature while transporting on an Away Team mission to explore the disappearance of the crew aboard the U.S.S. Yosemite. At first, no one believes Barclay until he begins displaying the physical manifestations of his encounter inside the transporter beam.

• • • •

"It should have been called realm of apprehension," laughed Story Editor Brannon Braga, who envisioned the episode as more horrifying than it eventually was. "The first three acts are fun and then the tech gets in the way. Certainly, it was my most personal episode to date. People around here say I am Barclay. I hate flying and that's where the idea came from. If I lived in the 24th century, I'd be afraid to transport, so I enjoyed exploring some of the deeper neuroses that Barclay had. All in all, it was nice doing a very indepth, one man character piece. The three most neurotic

• • • •

people on the staff have written Barclay. It was fun, I really enjoyed doing it. The tech was was a nightmare, but that's the way it goes. Sometimes things don't always turn out the way they read or people read them differently. I envisioned a scarier episode where the creatures in the transporter were a little more frightening, but then again what a tall order to the effects guys, 'make it amorphous, but terrifying.' What does that mean? It's easy to write that, but difficult to visualize. I just wanted you to feel scared with this guy and you never really did."

"I thought it was pretty good," said Co-Executive Producer Michael Piller. "I always like the Barclay shows. I think it's a perfectly valid fear to explore, whether you have a phobia about spiders or about being molecularly taken apart and put back together. As STAR TREK viewers we have come to take it for granted, but why shouldn't somebody be afraid to get into a transporter? I had always felt that there were too many similarities to that TWILIGHT ZONE where Shatner looks out and sees the creature on the wing of the plane ['Nightmare at 20,000 Feet']. I felt very strongly we needed to get the episode away from that, and I think we succeeded."

Said Jeri Taylor, "This

was an episode that a lot of people just didn't respond to and I don't know why. I thought it was a wonderful idea. I thought Brannon wrote a terrific script. It just seemed so perfect, Barclay with a transporter phobia just seemed like a marvelous marriage of something people can relate to today and in the future, technology. I just thought everything worked with maybe the exception of the visual effects. The explanation by the end really got painfully detailed. And it's that fine line you try to draw, if we don't say this is the audience going to be fairly confused and cheated because they don't understand it? But if we do say it, are they going to be overwhelmed by the words? We went one way in 'Time's Arrow II', and maybe we tried too hard to explain things in 'Realm of Fear', but it's hard to strike that back."

Everyone on staff welcomed the return of Dwight Schultz's Barclay. "He is the only person we could think of that would be right for it except a guest star," said Taylor. "It is just a little more interesting to have someone we know a little bit better than that. And we wanted to use Dwight more as a semi-regular this year. He's a wonderful actor, he likes the show and he likes doing the

show. I'd like to use him even more next year."

Episode #129
"Man of the People"

Written by Frank Abatemarco
Directed by Winrich Kolbe

Guest Starring:
Chip Lucia (Alkar), Susan French (Maylor), Stephanie Erb (Liva), Rick Scarry (Jarth), J.P. Hubbell (Ensign), Lucy Boryer (Ensign Janeway), George D. Wallace (Admiral)

Lumerian ambassador Alkar (Chip Lucia) and a woman he identifies as his mother, Maylor (Susan French), beam aboard the Enterprise to mediate a conflict. After Maylor's mysterious death, Alkar engages in a death ritual with Counselor Troi, using Deanna as the receptacle for his negative emotions while mediating the dispute. As a result, Troi transforms first into a jealous vamp and ultimately into a rapidly aging shrew.

••••

"The premise was basically 'The Picture of Dorian Gray'," said Story Editor Rene Echevarria of the script which was staff-written and rushed to the stage when "Relics'" filming was pushed back. "That was the soundbite. We were kind of stuck and we needed something very quickly. Since this was the only thing we had in the pipeline, we gangbanged it all writing an act and

Frank [Abatemarco] tied those acts together. It was a surprisingly good draft considering five different people wrote it. Some shows always do that. LA LAW writes everything as a staff like that and there's something compelling about it because overnight you have a first draft instead of someone pulling their hair out for two weeks."

"I would have done it differently," countered Brannon Braga. "I would have made it darker and much more a story about Troi's dark descent from the psychological point of view. A scene we all wanted to see was Troi giving therapy to a young ensign — but make it twice as long and twice as dark as the one that was filmed, and make it much more of a Hannibal Lecter thing. This was a case where Frank Abatemarco saw a different show. He was focusing in on the show as a Prime Directive issue and looking at the character of the guy who was using Troi as a receptacle. To me, that was the utterly incorrect instinct. After six years, who cares about Prime Directive issues? It's a STAR TREK cliché. It should have been all about Troi and he would have been the catalyst in two brief scenes. The first three acts were still fun. It was enjoyable to see Troi acting strange and dressing in skimpy outfits. There was some argument in the structuring sessions. Ultimately, Frank was the writer and he was given the opportunity to do it the way he wanted to do it, and it suffered because he's new to the show."

Science advisor Naren Shankar was also called on to explain how Troi is freed of the mental discharges of an alien ambassador in "Man of the People", in which she is transformed into an aged shrew.

"It was a difficult script and there are things in this that changed a number of times. My original idea was that this psychic link had set up some kind of conduit between the two of them, and my idea was to have them do something that wasn't mental, but something that was physical like his basically charging her up. If this was a one way pathway from this guy to Troi, the idea would be to put so much energy into Troi that she could force it backwards in the direction of the power transfer and overwhelm the guy and get rid of all that energy in her body. Some of that survived. I think it was Ron and Brannon who had the idea of Troi actually dying first, which was kind of a nice touch, to sever the link."

Offered director Winrich Kolbe, "I am very happy with it. There are obviously some problems with the script, but what intrigues me is that I took a script that had problems and came out with a damn good show. Marina was really terrific. She knew it was her show and was prepared for it. I think the only thing that I occasionally did was push her a little bit harder to become more of a vamp."

Said Sirtis of her transformation into a cosmic vixen, "I played it like these were underlying parts of Troi that she controlled or managed to suppress. And just looking in the mirror was all I needed to change. When I look in the mirror and see Troi, it's a very soft and gentle look. In the scene in Ten Forward where my hair was up, I saw Anne Bancroft in the mirror. I saw Mrs. Robinson and that's what I played. Basically, a lot of the performance is governed by the way that one looks. Some actors say they put the shoes for the characters on first and figure out the walk. I look in the mirror and play whatever I see in the mirror — especially when it's a make-up thing like in 'Man of the People', where the old person was a witch and that's who was in the mirror, so I played a witch."

Much of the staff is critical of the episode because of its hackneyed writing, but few would criticize the actress' strong performance. "Marina

• • • •

Nearly twenty years before returning to the bridge of the Enterprise in "Relics", James "Scotty" Doohan did so with writer Dorothy Fontana and George "Sulu" Takei at a '70s Star Trek *convention.*

brought more to it than might have happened in the hands of a lesser actress," said Ron Moore. "She's able to give life to a scene where sometimes we just have words on a page. She has to find something to do with them."

**Episode #130
"Relics"**

**Written by Ronald D. Moore
Directed by Alexander Singer**

Guest Starring:
James Doohan (Scotty), Lanei Chapman (Ensign Rager), Erick Weiss (Ensign Kane), Stacie Foster (Engineer Bartel), Ernie Mirich (Waiter), Majel Barrett (Computer Voice)

The Enterprise discov-

ers Montgomery Scott (James Doohan) suspended in a transporter beam aboard a Federation transport ship, and rescues him from a 75-year oblivion. Although at first Scotty is a man out of time, he proves vital in saving the Enterprise, one last time, from destruction inside a Dyson's sphere.

• • • •

Originally, Troi was going to ask Scotty if he wanted to know what happened to his colleagues aboard the Enterprise. "There was a line in a scene that got cut out between Troi and Scotty," said Producer Ronald D. Moore. "She said 'Would you like to

know what happened to all your friends and family?' and he said 'No, I'm not ready to hear that.' That was the closest allusion we were going to make. My thought is it would clutter it up a little bit to make direct references since once you bring up Bones and say that Mr. Spock is James Bond now and underground on Romulus, you have to talk about everybody else and we didn't want to say what happened to everybody else because we didn't want to lock ourselves into it."

Moore noted that several different scenarios were contemplated for ending the episode, although none of them were the rumored shuttling of Scotty to DEEP SPACE NINE. "We could just have sent him to a Starbase but that felt a little flat and we were never going to send him to a retirement community. There was one ending where Picard is on the bridge and Scotty is in engineering and Picard gives him the order to engage one more time and Scotty's got to run the engine room. But it felt like it wasn't going to be that dramatic. You press a button and that's it. Ultimately, there was some concern that we can't give our shuttles away either, but there's no money in the 24th century so what difference does it make? It's not like they're going to give him a bill for it, but they made me put in that line that it's a loan anyway."

Ultimately, the biggest challenge the producers faced was in visualizing the recreation of the Enterprise bridge which Moore had depicted differently in the story's conceptual stage.

"Originally I wanted to do some sequence on the holodeck with the original series characters in some way and we had talked briefly about an idea of doing it," said Ron Moore. "We were going to go down to the holodeck and have him actually interact with clips like the Diet Pepsi commercial with Bogart stuff.

We'd use a clip from the original series and have him look at them and talk to them or something, but that was very expensive and prohibitive and the more we could see that wasn't the right way to go. So I came up with this idea of the old bridge and there was a pause about that. They weren't sure they wanted to do it because it was going to be very, very expensive. The initial estimates to recreate that bridge were exorbitant, so there was a time there for a few days where it was sort of on the edge of whether we would be able to do it at all. But, you know, I think what happened is that a lot of people wanted to do that scene."

The first piece of the puzzle in recreating the original bridge set was laid by Production Designer Richard James during an early production meeting. "My initial reaction was what we wound up doing," said James. "I said if they could find a clip of the original where there was an empty bridge of the Enterprise, then we could take that film clip and do blue screen and I could just build a piece of the original to shoot the actors against. When Scotty walks in and sees an empty bridge and so forth, what he sees is a blue screen and then I explained that we could take the actor across

the blue screen and pick him up walking into the frame again and he'd be against the real set at that point."

"I said we couldn't build the bridge," recalled Supervising Producer David Livingston. "I'm sure I did. If I didn't, I should have. But that's when Richard brought up looking at the original show and seeing if we could get 'stock footage' off of it. That was like manna from heaven."

A clip from "This Side Of Paradise" was quickly located in which the spore-infected crew of the Enterprise deserts the ship, leaving Kirk alone on the bridge. "It was Kirk leaving the bridge through a turbo-lift that gave us enough footage of the empty original bridge that we could use as the blue screen plate to actually have our people walking in," said Livingston, who pointed out that the post-production team then repeated the clip over and over until they had enough footage to provide the establishing shot of the bridge. "People are literally walking into a shot that was created twenty-five years ago. That was kind of exciting for all of us. To realize that you can literally tie the two eras together so specifically, that was a kick for everybody."

"I didn't see how they were going to do it," said director Alexander Singer. "I assumed they had a complete bridge. When I was told they had one third of one part of it, I had to put on my thinking cap. I'd like to feel I'm a film-maker and that given anything to work with I probably can make it work if it's possible. No challenge has been as peculiar as this one, though. We had a monitor on the set and I worked from the monitor and I kept reliving the old STAR TREK deck although I was never on it as a director. It's not memorable to me, but all of the sudden I'm living in a place and I don't even have it in front of me to deal with. So the business of creating it was, to me, an enormous cinematic challenge. I had with me an art director and a visual effects director who in terms of their knowledge and sophistication could pace me very comfortably."

"I told Alex that we could take the actor walking across the blue screen and then pick him up walking into frame again, and he'd be against the real set at that point," explained Richard James, who constructed a pie-shaped wedge of the set which both Picard and Scotty were shot against in their scenes together. "I told him it becomes very restrictive but it will fill okay because I'll have the console out in the center, which he can walk past over

to his station. Then I said, 'For your reverses, I'll switch out the panels and it will be different artwork in there so you can do your reverses against the same set."

Literally replacing the artwork in the Enterprise bridge monitors allowed the production crew to move the panels around to the other side of the set to make it appear as though a larger circumference of the bridge set had been constructed when, in fact, it was a very small part of it. "I told him it will look like it's on the other side of the set so it will give the illusion that we literally did the full Enterprise bridge of the original series," said James. "We spent lots of time developing the color and looking at old clips and looking at anything we could get a hold of. There was nothing that existed in the way of drawings and we had to develop sketches from photographs. We developed our measurements by saying, 'This looks like it was that high,' and working from there. We really did look for detail and search for detail because we knew so many fans of the old series would be looking for it and it would mean a great deal to them."

The helm console was obtained by a fan who had once constructed a replica of the original bridge set, and still had many relics from his

endeavor. "There's a fan that Michael Okuda found that built the command chair and the helm," said Ron Moore. "Because we couldn't afford to build those he trucked it down in his van from Stockton. He rented it to us for probably a buck or whatever, and we used it on the set and then when that was done he put it back in his van and drove away with a unique souvenir of STAR TREK."

"Relics" is a tribute to the love that many of the production team still harbor for the original show. Many of the crew who had hid their manic enthusiasm for NEXT GENERATION's progenitor came out of the closest in order to mobilize for the production of the ambitious bridge sequence. "A lot of people put in a lot of extra effort and didn't get paid for it. They put in extra hours to make that possible and just bit the bullet because they wanted to do the scene," said Moore.

Greg Jein, who has constructed many of the show's miniatures, donated many of the button's found on the captain's chair and consoles. "We had a few buttons we had gotten from Jim Rugg a few years ago," said Jein. "They were just sitting in a closest and we found a good use for them that justified their existence again. STAR TREK never died. It's always fun to work on STAR

TREK. Even more so when it has tie-ins to the original classic that we all sort of grew up on. We had a lot of fun doing it, used a lot of our imagination and left over things."

When construction was finished and the final bridge set assembled, Moore was invited down to the set. "Michael Okuda gave me a call and said you've got to come down and see this before it's shot," recalled the writer. "I went down and sat there and got a tear in my eye. I sat in the captain's chair because it was so real. And then the day they were shooting I went down there and there was Jimmy on the bridge and then Majel came in to say 'hi' and then Bob Justman walked in."

Robert Justman, a producer on both the original show and the first season of NEXT GENERATION, was amazed at what he saw. "He came over and watched the scene and then said some very nice things to me about the writing of it," said Moore. "It was a like a time warp, standing on the bridge of the Enterprise with Bob Justman and Majel. I remember we were talking and when he first walked in he had his back to the set. He turned around and went, 'Oh, my God,' and he just looked at it. It was such an accurate re-creation he

couldn't believe it."

One gaffe Justman did detect was that the color of the carpet was off from that of the original series, but once lit properly it blended seamlessly with the shots from the original show.

Of course, the bridge wasn't the only complex creation for the episode. Moore's script also postulated a Dyson's Sphere, an entire enclosed solar system which the Enterprise becomes trapped in. Contributing to its construction was miniature-builder Greg Jein, who created the panels which were digitally replicated to visualize the enormous sphere. "We used some left over running ship parts to make the corridor from the interior of the Dyson's Sphere to the exterior, so the justification for hoarding all those things these last twenty odd years finally paid off," said Jein.

Ironically, the Dyson's Sphere concept had been kicked around by the writing staff for years for myriad potential B-stories in years past. "It was something that we were trying to put in for a long time and it became a standing joke," said Moore.

Added Naren Shankar, "I originally thought the interesting thing would be to make it a partially completed Dyson's Sphere because

there's some solar radiation thing that had gone on. It ended up being a complete Dyson's Sphere that was uninhabited. When Ron had written about the Dyson's Sphere in the teaser, he wrote tech and when I came I gave him the numbers for the size of it and he was shocked that it was so big. It was like the equivalent of four million earths, it's huge. If you build something the size of the sun's orbit, you're talking about a sphere with a diameter of two hundred million miles."

Several scenes from the show needed to be cut for length, including a lengthy scene in which Counselor Troi talks to Scotty about his feelings of being a man out of time. "That was purely a matter of how long the episode was and that happens a lot," said Marina Sirtis. "What didn't make sense was why I was kissing him at the end if she never met him. It's because the scene was cut out."

In the scene, Scotty becomes upset when he finds out that Troi is a counselor. "He didn't understand what she was there to do," explained Moore. "She says, 'Hi, I'm the ship's counselor.' He says, 'Oh yeah, what can I do for you?' She says, 'Well, I want to see how you're doing.' He says, 'Fine, the replicator is working.' He thinks she's the waiter or maid or something, and then finds out she's a psychologist and freaks out because he thinks Geordi sent her there. There was also a little bit more character stuff from Scotty about feeling out of a time and a place, and that he used to have a function on a ship like this and now he doesn't. That was a difficult thing for someone like him. But I don't think we missed it in the final cut, the story still works without it."

Said Story Editor Rene Echevarria of the completed episode. "All I can say was, as a fan I didn't even read it, I just watched it. It was delightful and the scene on the bridge was just wonderful. It just brought a tear to the eye and the Ten Forward scene, 'it is green' was a wonderful reference. The Dyson's Sphere I thought looked wonderful and the escape from it was a nice Millenium Falcon moment which was actually quite deftly done."

"I think it's the most enjoyment I've had writing an episode and it's the best I've done in a personal sense," offered Ron Moore. "It meant the most to me out of a lot of things I've written, because it resonates with my interest in STAR TREK from way back in that sense. I'm not sure if in the cold light of day that it's

the most brilliant thing I've ever written, but it just had a lot of meaning for me."

**Episode #131
"Schisms"**

**Teleplay by Brannon Braga
Story by Ronald Wilkerson
and Jean Matthias
Directed by Robert Wiemer**

Guest Starring:
Lanei Chapman (Ensign Rager), Ken Thorley (Mott), Scott T. Trost (Lieutenant Shipley), Angelo McCabe (Crewman), Angelina Fiordellisi (Kaminer), John Nelson (Medical Technician), Majel Barrett (Computer Voice)

Geordi's experiments with a new scanning system result in members of the crew being abducted and experimented on in a distant realm of subspace by a strange alien species. Riker is sent into the rupture in hopes of halting the aliens' incursions aboard the Enterprise.

••••

Said scripter Brannon Braga of the poetry reading in which Data delivers an ode to his cat, Spot, "That was a decision to do a cold teaser and the poetry reading was an idea we had been kicking around for quite a while. The thing that's great about the teaser is that it's still advancing the plot with Riker falling asleep, even though you don't think that's going to have anything to do with the story."

"I couldn't believe it because not only did it rhyme but it's technobabble and it also had something to say," said Brent Spiner, who grappled with the line reading. "It had a really sweet point of view towards the cat."

"It's a case where I wrote the most muddled, complex tech plot of all time," said Brannon Braga. "The entire fifth act had practically no dialogue in it, just tech. The first three acts were eerie, but the fourth act was a tech nightmare. I felt it was creepy and weird and terrifying. I like psychological suspense and terror, and when I had a chance to do that on STAR TREK I jumped at it. It seemed like a scary mystery to me until you see the aliens which look like monks. Unfortunately, the trailer also gave everything away, 'Aliens are using the Enterprise crew as human guinea pigs.' They showed everything during the coming attractions the week before, which was really annoying."

Said Braga, "I was chomping at the bit to do that story. I felt it was creepy and weird and terrifying and I am a horror fan. I like psychological suspense and terror and when I see a chance to do that on a show like STAR TREK, I want to do it. This story looked full of potential. It had some cliched elements to it;

getting kidnapped by aliens is not very fresh. I was more interested in those first four acts, the mystery and the weirdness and seeing our people losing their minds, which is not something you get to see very often. And that holodeck sequence I was looking forward to doing. I like using the holodeck as a tool to solve a mystery like in 'Identity Crisis.' It just seemed like a fun mystery to me and turned out to be sort of a scary episode."

Commented Naren Shankar, "It's funny what happens sometimes on our show. We ask for something that's really scary and we don't get something that's very scary. The bar in 'Tapestry' was spookier and more otherworldly than the aliens in 'Schisms.' It's so difficult to tell on a production of this size the way things are going to turn out when you put them together. Personally, I thought the aliens would have been better in 'Schisms' if we had never seen their faces. Whatever you saw would have been an anti-climax. I would have been happier to see them cloaked in shadow. Dramatically, that would have been better choice. In general, 'Schisms' ran the same difficulty, that 'Realm of Fear' did. We had a very interesting story and we kept putting off the tech till the end of the

show and it just snowballed. I could not even begin to tell you how difficult it was for Brannon to go through that and even for the sake of clarity it didn't turn out very well. You had tetyon particle emissions, you had leading to this and a honeycombed multidimensional structure of subspace and tertiary manifolds and blah, blah, blah. We turn on the shields and surround it with a subspace and they're all logical points and trails and lead legitimate places. The problem is when you get them all at once, it's impossible to absorb new information. You don't know what to do with it and you lose the thread completely and that's what happened in 'Schisms'."

The show, like first season's "Conspiracy", is open-ended, thus indicating that the 'Schisms' menace could return. "That was intentional," explained Braga. "Mike Piller didn't want to do it and Rick Berman was on the fence about it, but I really wanted to do it. Mike thought it was corny and he may be right. I wanted to do something where it wasn't resolved and where maybe we could see these guys again. I think there's something very creepy about a squirmy wormy thing shooting out into space and you don't even know what it was. At least in the script, I described it

as a snake of energy."

"It was a funny idea to do COMMUNION on the Enterprise, since we deal with aliens all the time," agreed Rene Echevarria. "We wanted to do something really different and alien like 'Time's Arrow', but they were very expensive so we couldn't do anything really unusual. It was a mystery, so I think it really hinged on not knowing what was going on. Unfortunately, the preview from the previous week told far too much."

"That was kind of like CLOSE ENCOUNTERS OF THE THIRD KIND," said Richard James of his thoughts during the first production meetings. "I really saw that from some of the descriptions that you hear people talk about in there abduction experiences."

James worked closely with make-up supervisor Michael Westmore and Costume Designer Robert Blackman to find the appropriate look for the eerie, alien domain described in Brannon Braga's script. "The room sort of just drops off into blackness with bright light and there's no detail," he said. "Everything was kind of fuzzy and that was the set. I used fiberglass, which I had seen cut on a sawhorse in the plaster shop, and I told them that's what I want my set to look like; furry and fuzzy-like. I wanted to give the feel-

"True Q" guest star Olivia d'Abo as seen with Arnold Schwarzenegger in Conan-The Destroyer *(photo copyright © 1984 Universal City Studios, Inc.)*

ing that it was maybe an insect kind of civilization and that these might be a hybrid of insects and grasshoppers, and it was all done against a black background."

Said David Livingston of the complicated shoot, "I love the way that Bob Wiemer shot it with the wide angle lens. He made it look very odd, and he did some very unusual and strange camera moves across Jonathan and that device he was restrained on. I thought it was very

bizarre. He doesn't hold anything back. He's got a very strong visual imagination, and I respect his work. A lot of it is the luck of the draw for a director too, but he's gotten some scripts that have allowed him to be able to do that kind of odd, unusual thing. If you can't do it on STAR TREK, where can you do it?"

Despite Wiemer's impressive direction, Livingston acknowledged that the episode was impacted on by budget exigencies. "One

problem was we couldn't afford a lot of these aliens because they were expensive," he said. "Bob Wiemer had to be very judicious in shooting them, and also revealing them, because we didn't want to see a lot of them. We couldn't afford to build a complete set so it went off into limbo because it was too expensive. I thought what Bob Wiemer and Richard James did to solve those problems was very creative."

• • • •

Episode #132
"True Q"

Written by Rene Echevarria
Directed by Robert Scheerer

Guest Starring:
John DeLancie (Q), Olivia d'Abo (Amanda), John P. Connolly (Lote)

An Enterprise intern named Amanda (CONAN THE DESTROYER's Olivia d'Abo) is revealed as a member of the Q continuum. Q (John DeLancie) himself pays another unwanted visit onboard, where he confides to Picard that Amanda's parents were actually Q. Amanda must choose between joining him among the Q — or death!

• • • •

Bought as a premise from Matt Corey, a North Carolina high school student, Echevarria immediately latched onto the storyline when he found an intern reading the spec script submission. "I thought it was charming when she told me the nugget that a young kid finds out he's a Q. I told Jeri and she thought it was a great idea and immediately bought the premise."

After taking an unintentional hiatus for a season and leaving viewers wondering, "Where's Q?", the omnipotent super being was back with a vengeance in three STAR TREK stories over the course of the last television season, terroriz-

ing the crew of the Enterprise twice as well as paying a visit on the new residents of Deep Space Nine.

John DeLancie, who portrays the miser of mirth and malevolence, admits he shared fan concerns when he failed to wreak havoc fifth season. "After four years of some sort of continuity, I heard there was a script," said DeLancie. "I talked to Jonathan Frakes one day when I was at the studio, and he said, 'You're going to be the third show from January' and gave me a strong indication I was going to be working. When it didn't happen, I thought it was odd, but in our business what we think should happen and shouldn't happen is of very little consequence to what the people who are really running the show think."

In fact, the people running the show very much wanted to have Q back fifth season, but they were having their own problems trying to lick two difficult script premises — "Q-Olympics" and "Q Makes Two" — neither of which made it to the screen sixth season.

In "Q Makes Two," a story that made the rounds of the writing staff for nearly a year, Q creates a duplicate of the Enterprise and the crew. "What made it so difficult was we doubled the entire crew

and I thought the whole concept was flawed," said Story Editor Brannon Braga. "The way I thought it should have gone was Q doubled them and there was one uniform characteristic that's different about all of the crewmembers; they're all evil, greedy or something. That seems simplistic, but I think it could have worked dramatically in a one hour episode. What we tried to do was give each character several psychological characteristics that were different and none of them were the same. So suddenly you have to delineate 12 characters, none of whom are the original. It was so impossibly complicated that we had to write a little chart on the board while were breaking to keep clear visually for us who was who. My suggestion as a joke was we should do a 7-11 tie-in where the audience could go to 7-11 and buy a little chart to keep clear who was who in the episode."

Continued Braga, "There was a sense of doom from the moment we started, 'Q Makes Two.' I think we broke it three times. Rene wrote two drafts and it was ultimately abandoned. It's an interesting notion that Q comes onboard and Picard's saying people are inherently good and we have managed to get rid of our darker elements in the 24th century and we're

An early concept for "True Q" would have pit the Enterprise against an exact duplicate of itself (comic book cover copyright © 1990 DC Comics).

better people. Q says so you don't think you have dark components and you think you're better without them, well I'm going to show you a thing or two and so he extracts the darker components and puts them into doubles. The clean, good components suffer and so do the darker components and neither functions without the other. We see that dramatically, but for some reason we made it more complex than it needed to be. It's a show that could still work. The image in my mind that we never really got to was the two Enterprises shooting at each other, that's what you want to see. Someday maybe, but until then 'Q Makes Two' will never see the light of day."

After 'Q Makes Two' was abandoned, a premise was purchased from a young high school student that was turned into "True Q", in which a young human intern aboard the Enterprise, played by Olivia d'Abo, must accept that she is a Q and join the continuum or promise never to use her powers.

"'Q Makes Two' was a debacle and it plunged us into a nightmare of having to get 'Man of the People' ready," noted Jeri Taylor. "When we started in on another Q episode, I was a little apprehensive, to say the least. I thought, why are we going back into this so quickly? But this was a delightful premise which came our way from a young man who wrote a spec script and had had notions of playing the part of the young person himself, but we made it a female and ruined that for him. It was definitely a high concept, wonderful idea. This was, in contrast to the other Q episode, one that I knew would work. It just felt right."

Although the premise bears some resemblance to season one's "Hide & Q", in which Riker is offered the power of the Q and ordered by Picard not to use it, writer Rene Echevarria didn't overly concern himself with the similarities. "The premise was similar, but a lot of first season stuff we try not to feel bound by because a lot of it wasn't well executed and this was just a much better story," said the story editor. "Her reaction to it was more believable and it was a deliberate choice not to raise the question of Riker's situation since some of those choices and things he went through were so strange that it was better to just hope a lot of people didn't see it."

One of the writing staff's goals for the new season was to return the character of Q to his early malevolence and try not to portray him as the whimsical mirth-maker that he had become in such episodes as the lighthearted "Q-pid" and certain moments of "Deja Q."

"I felt the proportions were about right to me," said Echevarria. "He had some very funny bits, like where he said that the study of humans 'is not a very challenging field of study, I grant you,' which was Jeri's line. The problems with Q stories is that people often just use him to get the machinery rolling; he doubles us [as in 'Q Makes Two'], but why is it a Q story? Why isn't it personal? This *was* personal and he was malevolent. We tried to play some mystery for a while. He was testing her and he just pops up in the staff meeting. We sometimes wonder how effective anything is when so much is given away in the coming attractions — people knew it was a Q show. But I was very happy."

Ironically, Q's most malevolent moments in "True Q", in which he threatens to terminate the girl, came about during the actual filming of the episode. Up until that point, the subplot hadn't even existed.

"It gave it a sense of momentum and import," said Echevarria. "Michael came up with the idea that Q had been sent to kill her very late in the process, it was too late to do a major rewrite. Most of Act Four had been filmed, which had to do with her being in love with Riker. Several key scenes had been filmed and could not be changed. That shouldn't happen but in this case it did. It was pretty heinous of him to be willing to kill this girl, but I think in a strange way it worked very nicely to have the audience have that knowledge and in the meantime they're seeing a very light, romantic story and are saying, 'Doesn't she realize what's at stake here?' That worked in a strange way very well. I doubt we would have written in that way. Michael found a way, very cleanly, in Act 3 where Q is walking down the corridor and a Q shadow appears to give Act 4 a much more sinister undedrtone. If we had more time Act 4, probably would have been very different. We probably wouldn't have done the Riker romance stuff. There would have been other beats we would have played."

Said John DeLancie, "After the one in which I lose my powers, 'Deja Q', I had said to them this is as far as we should go in this area for a while. Let's make the next one have a little bit of bite to it. Then came the Robin Hood one and I tried quite a bit actually to bend the words and the story to make it as malevolent as possible, but it had quite a bit of a fantasy quality to it. It really didn't lend itself to that 'mad, bad and dangerous to know' quality, but I tried to make it that. When I came back to do 'True Q' and it was kind of Q babysits, I tried to put malevolence in places there, but that didn't really lend itself again. The thing is that I remember having said somewhere along the line, 'Kill her.' They all said 'My god, no, no, no' and I said, 'Why not?' And they said, 'John, you're just being Q-like' and I said 'Well, yeah, you got it. Come in and kill her, assassin.' It's a hard ball nature that I would like to try and find again, but I can't do it within the context of birthday parties and babysitting and stuff like that. It's something you need to have the set up for. I would have liked to have taken it one step further where she was killed."

Said Taylor of the last-minute rewriting to accommodate Q's more notorious nature, "If I had my druthers, we would have every script ready before prep. That never happens. We're usually doing a fair amount of rewriting in prep and we try to have it locked before it's shooting, but that doesn't always happen. It's certainly not the only episode which we were rewriting during the shooting. In fact, we maybe did less on that than we did on some others. That's always kind of dangerous to start playing around with that, but it really only affected the scene where Q talked to the shadow — the end scene where Amanda is made to realize that he is going to kill her — so it wasn't like it rippled through the entire script, it was not a profound change and certainly was for the better."

Ultimately, "True Q" presented many challenges to writer Rene Echevarria, who was writing the teleplay as a member of the writing staff. "It turned out to be a very tough story and it was hard to write the scenes in which our people tried to give this person advice. I think we came up with some nice moments. The chase on the Enterprise that ends up on the hull when she summons the image of her family, things like that. But everytime we tried to write Beverly's advice to her and things like, 'I don't care if your omnipotent, you have to do this experiment', it was very hard."

Episode #133
"Rascals"

Teleplay by Allison Hock
Story by Ward Botsford & Diana Dru Botsford and Michael Piller
Directed by Adam Nimoy

Guest Starring:

Whoopi Goldberg (Guinan), Brian Bonsall (Alexander), David Tristan Birkin (Young Picard), Isis Jones (Young Guinan), Caroline Junko King (Young Keiko), Mike Gomez (Lurin), Tracey Walter (Berik), Michael Snyder (Morta), Colm Meaney (O'Brien), Michelle Forbes (Ensign Ro), Megan Parlen (Young Ro), Morgan Nagler (Kid #1), Hana Hatae (Molly), Rosalind Chao (Keiko), Majel Barrett

(Computer Voice)

Picard, Guinan (Whoopi Goldberg), Ensign Ro (Michelle Forbes) and Keiko (Rosalind Chao) are transformed into children during a shuttle accident, but nonetheless prove vital in saving the Enterprise from Ferengi mercenaries who attempt to take over the starship.

• • • •

"It was not my favorite assignment and it was a difficult show to write," admitted Ron Moore. "I felt that this time I hadn't dodged the bullet fast enough and once I got stuck with it, I put aside my feelings about it and tried to do the best that I could. I made a real attempt to find things within it that would work and to dig a little deeper to find some character moments that I thought would play."

A day that Naren Shankar doesn't remember fondly is when he needed to bring all his scientific and technical knowledge to bear in an attempt to explain one of the show's silliest script premises. "'Rascals' was not a happy day," he said of the episode in which Picard, Ro Laren, Keiko and Guinan are transformed into children. "Do we have to talk about this?"

Ron Moore, who did the final production rewrite on the show, was put in the unenviable position of having to explain what had created their

Michelle Forbes portrayed Ensign Ro for the last time in "Rascals" (photo copyright © 1993 Karen Witkowski).

ed biological theory that the fetus goes through a development that is parallel to the evolution of development, starting out as a fish and finally becoming a human, going through the whole evolutionary cycle, which is silly. The idea was that we were saying there was a little homonucleus inside your body that shows how you are at each stage of your life. I was saying we can't be doing this. The problem was that it was virtually impossible to come up with a sensible explanation and so we kind of did a lot of hand waving on this episode."

When asked about the *deus ex machina* in which the crew is returned to normal thanks to their pattern being stored in the transporter's pattern buffers, Shankar replied, "Let's not even talk about it. Let's just forget that ever happened. For Adam, that was a helluva way to make a directorial debut. Directing kids is not easy under any circumstances. I think the boy who played Picard was tough because the biggest problem was the voices were not right and it was difficult to see. It's so hard to cast kids. The young Ro was phenomenal. She was the one person in that cast I thought was terrific. In a lot of ways she reminded me of Christina Ricci [ADDAMS FAMILY]. This girl who played

condition. Being a self-described "liberal arts moron," Moore consulted with Shankar and later the discussions made their way into staff meetings. "We were talking about the show and we started talking about whether there could be this sequence in the genes that shows how big they were when they were kids. I said, 'You know what you're doing, this the old antogeny recapitulates philogeny argument.' There was dead silence and I said, 'Am I the only person here who knows what this means?'"

Explained Shankar, "There's that ancient discredit-

• • • •

the young Ro showed a lot of poise and gravity and she was the one I most believed was the person she was supposed to be. The girl who played Whoopi had played her as a young girl in SISTER ACT."

As many fans suspected, the actress was indeed dubbed. "When Michael Piller and I heard the pitch, we thought it was a great idea," recalled Jeri Taylor of the episode. "Of course, he and I were the only people who felt that way. I thought to see the incipient little personalities of our people was a fetching idea. Ron made it work and the young girl playing Ro was fantastic. We seriously suggested to Rick and Michael that we keep her on since we never saw Ro get changed back at the end and we knew that Michelle Forbes was not going to be around anymore. They looked at us like we were absolutely insane. Where else but on STAR TREK would you do something like that? She gets transformed into a little person and she flies the ship. I think it would have been great."

One thing Taylor disagreed with Piller on was the adversaries who take over the ship which the pint-sized Picard must confront. "I always thought it might work better if there were a more sinister kind of element to the story pulling against the frivoli-

ty of the children," said Taylor. "Michael felt that the Ferengi were going to play more comfortably with the children because they are somewhat comedic themselves and it just wouldn't be believable that our children could defeat the Cardassians or the Romulans or some other lethal antagonist. I think it just stretched credibility too far. He was probably right, but it does kind of gall me to think that five Ferengi can take over the Enterprise. It was a big one to swallow, but we tried."

Episode #134
"A Fistful of Datas"

Teleplay by Robert Hewitt Wolfe and Brannon Braga
Story Robert Wolfe
Directed by Patrick Stewart

Guest Starring:
Brian Bonsall (Alexander), John Pyper-Ferguson (Eli Hollander), Joy Garrett (Annie), Jorge Cervera (Bandito), Majel Barrett (Computer Voice)

When the holodeck malfunctions, Worf, Alexander and Troi find themselves facing off against the specter of many gunmen as duplicates of Data take over the computer-generated town, turning Alexander's holodeck fantasy into a most dangerous game indeed. In order to rescue Alexander from Data's evil gunman, Eli, Worf must face him in a shootout in

the town square.

••••

"It was originally called WESTERN STORY on my contracts," said writer Robert Hewitt Wolfe. "Then it was called THE GOOD, THE BAD AND THE KLINGON, which was its title for a while. At the very last minute I thought of A FISTFUL OF DATAS."

"I had the chance to play five or six characters in a show and Patrick directed, which made it additionally fun," said Brent Spiner. "It's certainly the most fun episode I've ever had to do and I'd like to do a show next season called FOR A FEW DATAS MORE."

"We hadn't done a holodeck malfunctioning story in three seasons, which is a perfectly good track record," said Naren Shankar. "It was a lighthearted show and it was a nice show. People love 'Shore Leave' and this show reminds me of that in a way. It's a western fantasy in a holodeck with a kid and there are some genuinely great moments. I think it's hilarious that Brannon, who doesn't know anything about westerns, wrote it and Patrick, an Englishman, directed it."

"Patrick and I were standing there together talking about the episode when one of their trams came by," recalled production designer Richard

James of a location scouting jaunt to Universal Studios. "I was laughing because Patrick had his back to the tram but the tour guide was pointing out something and all these people recognized Patrick and started taking pictures. I said to him that he had been recognized and he said, 'You know, Richard, 20 years ago I was one of those people on the tram.'"

"It's scary isn't it?" said David Livingston of Englishman Stewart directing the western. "What does he know about westerns? He has Robin Hood and stuff like that. Patrick did a wonderful job. He had a great time. He was Sergio Leone out there or Clint Eastwood, and Brent chewed every piece of scenery in sight and there wasn't any left by the time he got done. I think he played more characters in that then he ever played because he was everywhere. We shot that at Warner Bros. Burbank Studios. out in the valley. It was great high-concept."

"This was a holodeck romp and it should be light and fun," said Brannon Braga. "I pumped up the Data acting bizarre angle a little bit from the original draft. It was a lot of fun to come up with a good gag for the end. What was going to be special about this gunfight? What was going to make it STAR TREK? Suddenly,

that's where it needed to be STAR TREK again when you have Worf defeating the holodeck villain in a special STAR TREK way and I thought the force field was fun as was the character's reactions to it. The one thing I miss was that in my draft there was a Data, bandito Alexander scene that was inspired by 'Ransom of Red Chief', where basically you have the bandito holding Alexander in the cave. Data as the bandito with Alexander tied up, but the show was long and we had to cut it. It was a smooth process. Patrick and I talked a lot. Mainly about the final gun battle because it was very difficult to produce."

"A couple of times I had to really scream at Brannon to put some gags into it, but they worked out pretty well," said Naren Shankar of the teleplay. "It was a fun script. I was a little surprised that it didn't get as positive a reaction to the story as I would have expected. I loved it, I thought it was a very good show. I think it has one of the single greatest end shots I've ever seen on our show [the Enterprise flying into the sunset]. That's great. Some people get possessive of the show and it sometimes interferes with their enjoyment, I think, when they think it's too light for STAR TREK. You've got to be able to take a step back and

just enjoy it. It was a light-hearted show, there was no world bashing, there weren't huge problems and it was just a nice show. People love 'Shore Leave', I love it. This show reminds me of that in way. There's a little bit of a problem with the Enterprise, nothing major. I think 'Shore Leave' had stronger emotional ties initially because people were getting killed down there when their fantasies were getting out of control. But in many ways it's very similar and both are very enjoyable. You have to take it the way it's intended. It's a western fantasy in a holodeck with a kid and there are some genuinely great moments. When he goes in there the first time and the outlaw says, 'What are you going to do, arrest me?' and Worf knocks him out and Alexander says it's too easy and then Worf gets into the bar fight, is inspired writing."

"I'm not a big fan of westerns to be honest," confessed Marina Sirtis, the British actress who takes on the role of the Durango Kid in Alexander's holodeck simulation. "The whole week I had to contend with Michael Dorn telling me I was holding the gun like a girl and I would say, 'Well, Michael, I am a girl' and he'd say, 'Yeah, but you're supposed to be Clint Eastwood' so he'd give me gun holding lessons. It was play-time, that episode was let's have fun and we did.

"Maybe to our surprise," added Sirtis, "Patrick turned out to be a really, really wonderful director. We thought that because he's such a fabulous actor he would be constantly giving us acting notes and saying, 'This is how I would play the part' and he didn't do that at all. He behaved himself very well and was a joy to work for. It was a tough episode. Maybe some of the Americans thought why is a Brit directing the western, but I thought he did a great job and Brent was unreal in that show. I thought he was fabulous."

In the original draft of the script by Robert Hewitt Wolfe, Alexander's motivation for bringing Worf and Troi together on the holodeck is to forment a romantic relationship between the Klingon and the Betazoid. "My only regret is that element somehow did not end up on screen," said Shankar. "Alexander wrote a holodeck program to get Worf and Troi to fall in love with each other and everybody was going to play a part in this program. Troi was supposed to be the saloon girl, but when she goes into the program, she says, 'I don't want to be the saloon girl' and she changes her part and becomes the gun-slinger. That throws a monkey

wrench to Alexander's plan. This was a story element that was the emotional heart of the story and I don't know what happened to it. I loved it and thought it was a great idea and was sweet and funny. You can still see pieces of it as a story. Alexander gets really upset when Troi wants to be the gun-slinger and at the end when the saloon girl jumps into Worf's arms and kisses him, that was the end of the program because that's what he had planned for Troi."

Episode #135
"The Quality of Life"

Written by Naren Shankar
Directed by Jonathan Frakes

Guest Starring:
Ellen Bry (Dr. Farallon), David Windsor (Transporter Chief Kelso), Majel Barrett (Computer Voice)

A scientist, Dr. Farallon (Ellen Bry), who has created a revolutionary method for mining using a solar particle fountain, has invented an even more miraculous tool: the exo-comp, whose computerized brain allows it to learn. This leads Data to the conclusion that the mechanical devices are a life form, thus pitting him against Riker who wants to sacrifice the automotons to save Picard and Geordi.

• • • •

"They were originally supposed to be called meta-

comps which I liked better," said Naren Shankar of what actor/director Jonathan Frakes calls 'the little piggies.' "The idea was it stood for metamorphic computer, which is what they were, but apparently metacomp is a company somewhere so our legal department said we should change it. The problem was coming up with a lifeform that was sufficiently alien so that people wouldn't automatically think that they were alive, but where Data's unique insight into the machine — because he's a machine himself — would give him the edge that he needed to make the realizations he needed to make."

The episode prevented many pitfalls for newly promoted staff writer, Naren Shankar. "To be quite honest, I personally feel I pulled it off," said Shankar. "The main problem was a story problem. You get to a certain point where you have to step back and say by the logic of the arguments, is practically anything going to be considered a lifeform? That's where the real pitfall of this episode was. Some of the arguments Data is making just aren't that strong. You can apply very similar ideas to bacteria or unicellular life forms of various kinds. According to his argument, these must be an intelligent life form too, but are they? I don't think so. Who's to say where you draw the line? It's almost like I found myself coming down on a right-to-life argument in certain ways — and I definitely didn't want to find myself there. It's always good as an exercise to argue the opposite point of something. I'm very strongly pro-choice and writing a show like this is in some ways difficult because I didn't necessarily agree with it all the time, but you still have to make a strong case for it and I think in a lot of ways that was accomplished and in other ways it was not."

Said director Frakes, "The only problem I had with 'Quality of Life' is that it was short and they added the poker scene at the beginning. I was amazed that they refused to resolve it at the end. Either Gates should have been a brunette or we should have been sitting in the chair about to be shaved. I don't know why they would lay it out as a red herring and not have it pay off in some way — as if no one was watching the show."

"I sleep a little better between days," added Frakes of his more recent directorial assignments. "The first couple of episodes I did I was so nervous and so aware of how over-prepared I needed to be that I worked myself into not sleeping obsessively. I've done six now and I feel a little

more confident."

After last year's complicated time-loop installment, "Cause & Effect", "Quality of Life" was less of a challenge for the director who had grappled with shooting several of the same scenes differently for his last assignment. "It was a little heavy on technobabble, but all things considered I think that show came out quite well," said Frakes. "A lot of the credit goes to Brent as usual and LeVar and our guest star, Ellen Bry, who was up to it. Unlike most of the actresses I read, she seemed to be able to handle the language which in other actresses' mouths sounded dull. She somehow had passion about it and was able to deliver the lines with the same kind of alacrity as Brent and LeVar did on a daily basis."

The one concern that everyone had in shooting the episode was making the exocomps credible. As flying mechanical computer tools, the exocomps needed to appear functional and also sympathetic as a life form when Data contends that the automotons are sentient.

"We had a lot of discussions about that," said David Livingston. "The question was how to personify them. How to give it some character to make it so you identify and sympathize with it. We went through a lot of designs. Rick

Sternbach went through a lot of concepts until we finally all said, 'Yeah, this thing has some character to it.' Then the question was how to avoid spending eight million dollars on the opticals. We ended up doing some of it on the set by lifting them up and down on a pole and doing a little screen work. I think it was quite successful in that regard. Peter Lauritson and wanted to do a shot of it going down the tunnel because he thought that it was really important and I put the kibosh on it. I said, 'No, we can't afford it.' Well, Peter found the money and did the shot and he was right. It paid off. It was really fun to see it zipping down the tunnel."

In visualizing the exocomps, Livingston recalled all too well how easy it is to botch a physical effect, as the production team did on the "Farpoint" pilot. "I remember meeting with Rick Berman on a Sunday because I had gone to the stage to look at the progress we were making on this technical set where we had these arms that reached out and grabbed some of the crew members from The Enterprise. I was so concerned about it that I called Rick to come down and look at it with Herman Zimmerman. We looked at it, and it was bad, real bad. We tried to make some alterations and it was no longer bad, just grossly mediocre. In the final version of the film, most of it is cut out."

Episode #136
"Chain of Command, Part I"

Teleplay by Ron Moore
Story by Frank Abatemarco
Directed by Robert Scheerer

Guest Starring:
David Warner (Gul Madred), Ronny Cox (Captain Jellico), Natalija Nogulich (Admiral Nechayev), John Durbin (Gul Lemec), Lou Wagner (Solok)

When hostilities flare with the Cardassians, Picard is reassigned on a secret mission with Worf and Dr. Crusher to investigate reports the Cardassians are developing a metagenic weapon on Celtris III. Meanwhile, Captain Edward Jellico (Ronny Cox) of the USS Cairo is assigned to the Enterprise as its new captain, where he makes many enemies — including Commander Riker.

• • • •

Originally intended to be a single episode, Michael Piller made the suggestion that the show be split into two for a number of reasons. Ironically, the foremost consideration behind the decision was financial and not dramatic — although it manifested itself as one of the most astute decisions of the year, jump-starting the floundering sixth season.

"We needed to save money," said Jeri Taylor. "We were in budget trouble and Michael said, 'You know, I think what we could do is make this a two-parter. Have Picard captured and then make it an episode about his relationship with his torturer that takes place in one room. It's a fascinating two-person play and we'll get another episode out of it that way and we'll save a lot of money that will bring us even with the budget.

"The fundamental pitch the gang came in with was you have Picard on a mission and a new captain comes in and how does the crew react to the new captain," said Michael Piller of the original premise. "Jeri's idea was to cast Ronny Cox and I thought that worked out very well. They wanted to put Picard in a real rugged adventure story and they talked about this mission and he gets caught by the Cardassians and we rescue him and that's about it. I said this is a really good idea, but I was also looking to save money and I realized this might serve two masters. I knew if we divided it into two parts and made the first part the mission and then Picard gets caught, instead of that up in an hour, you put Patrick Stewart in a room with another great actor and you do the tor-

ture show. You call up Amnesty International and you get their cooperation, which is very important to Patrick, and you build a relationship between two men; one who is trying to beat the other and the other who is trying to survive."

"Chain of Command's" evolution from what would have been a simple action / adventure show into one of the most significant shows of the season, is a dramatic example of how the perpetual money woes on the show don't necessarily impact on the show adversely and can often serve as a source of creative inspiration.

"I think that money and creativity have never really gone hand in hand when it comes to STAR TREK," said Rick Berman. "Episodes like 'Measure of A Man' was one of our cheapest episodes and one of our best, but an episode like 'Yesterday's Enterprise' was quite expensive and it was wonderful. 'Chain of Command' was a very inexpensive episode and one of the greats."

Added Michael Piller, "Ultimately, the victory for Picard is just surviving. We made the decision early on that we couldn't say that Captain Picard was such a great man that he would not break under torture, because that would be doing a great disservice to everybody in the human rights struggle who has

In "Chain of Command Part 2" Patrick Stewart gave one of his strongest performances ever as a tortured Captain Picard (photo copyright © 1993 Karen Witkowski).

broken. Nobody can resist torture. Anybody who wants to get you to speak will get you to talk if they're willing to do the hideous things necessary. There had to be a different kind of victory. I can't imagine a better show than 'Chain of Command, Part II' and it had no tricks or whiz bang stuff and it was one of the least expensive shows of the season. David Warner was sensational and Patrick Stewart was even better. I don't think there's been a better show in the history of this series, and certainly there has not been a better hour of television on this year."

Originally, "Chain of Command" had been considered as the first DEEP SPACE NINE crossover, an idea that was vetoed by Rick Berman. "We were going to go to DS9 and that's how we were going to get to this planet in the show," recalled Rene Echevarria. "The Enterprise was going to come to DS9 and get a ship. The scene with the Ferengi was written for Quark

and I don't think Ron changed a word except the guy's name. We were going to borrow one of their Runabouts which Jellico was going to ask for and it just didn't work out. Rick wanted to wait a little longer before doing a crossover, it was less expensive, because if you go to DEEP SPACE NINE you have to use at least one of their regulars."

Ironically, the scene in which Picard, Worf and Dr. Crusher obtain passage to Celtris III was shot on the DEEP SPACE NINE soundstages by doing a small redress on one of the corners of the Promenade. "It was difficult to shoot," said Supervising Producer David Livingston, "because if you moved the camera around too much you'd see Quark's bar."

Driven by two powerhouse performances, "Chain of Command" ultimately pits Picard against a provocative Cardassian interrogator who seeks to break the Captain's spirit rather than obtain information.

"I think that it showed Patrick off at his best and David Warner is someone who I've always been a huge fan of," said Rick Berman. "I remember Patrick introducing me to David Warner at a party at Leonard Nimoy's home once, and it was great to bring them together. I think we had

RoboCop's Ronny Cox (affectionately known as Dick in that film) took command of the Enterprise as Captain Jellico in the two-part "Chain of Command" (photo copyright © 1987 Orion Pictures).

something to say about man's inhumanity to man and we got a lot of criticism for it being a little bit too graphic. I think we kept it from being as graphic as it could have been. I just think it was a wonderful piece of television."

"I wanted to write a captain for the Enterprise who would be genuinely different than Picard, but somebody we could also buy as captain," said Ron Moore of Captain Edward Jellico. "He was a pain in the ass and some people didn't like him, but he had redeeming qualities to him and was a different sort of man with a different kind of drive. But, you would believe that if

worse came to worse, if Picard never came back from Closest Land, the audience could see him as Captain."

Added Rene Echevarria, "Jellico was very much Ron's creation. I think he used some experiences of his own from ROTC. He was intended to be more likable and the demands of the story pushed Jellico in another direction. You were intended to see that he was a very different kind of man than Picard. He would go into Ten Forward, and as long as everything was perfect and his way, he'd slap you on the back and have a drink with you and sing a drinking song. A lot of that was cut for time. There was a

scene where Picard was still onboard and comes into Ten Forward and sees his people yukking it up with Jellico and realizes that Jellico is a lot more accessible and it's a moment where he wonders about giving up his ship and if he is so easily replaceable."

"Chain Of Command" boasted some of the series' most ambitious stage effects during the sixth season, when Picard, Worf and Dr. Crusher infiltrate a Cardassian outpost by making their way through a maze of caves on the alien planet. Livingston reluctantly gave in to the requests of director Robert Scheerer to keep a scene of the three scaling a large rock face.

• • • •

"Bob is so prepared and together that he makes it seem effortless," said Livingston. "He pleaded to do the repelling down scene and I kept fighting it because I thought it was too much money. He brought me over to the stage with Richard James, and Merri Howard and I stood there and he explained what he wanted to do. We allowed him to do it, and I'm really glad we did. It paid off. It's exciting stuff, and it's all shot on the sound stage. We built just enough to surround the actors. There was literally a foot above their heads and not much on the sides and the rest was a matte painting."

Said Richard James of the winding caverns on the Cardassian planet, Celtris Three. "We had to create a maze so that they could reuse corridors over and over and you didn't realize, so you shoot it from one direction and shoot it from another direction to make it look like they have much more set than they really do."

Episode #137
"Chain of Command, Part II"

Written by Frank Abatemarco
Directed by Les Landau

Guest Starring:
Ronny Cox (Captain Jellico), John Durbin (Gul Lemec), David Warner (Gul Madred), Heather Lauren Olson (Jil Orra)

Picard is brutally tortured by a Cardassian inquisitor, Gul Madred (David Warner), in hopes of obtaining the Federation's defense strategy against a Cardassian takeover of a disputed quadrant. On the Enterprise, Captain Jellico (Ronny Cox) attempts to stop the invasion by using Riker to mine the hulls of Cardassian warships.

• • • •

A film that proved an important reference point for the episode was "Closest Land," the little-seen 87 minute drama with Alan Rickman as a seductively low-key, but gleeful torturer and Madeline Stowe, a writer of childrens books which are believed to be subversive, as his political prisoner. The film was written and directed by Radha Bharadwaj and features scenes of psychological and physical abuse, including a moment when Rickman electrocutes Stowe by attaching wires to her genitals. The film is set in an unnamed country and boasts elaborate production and costume design by DRACULA's Oscar Award winning costume designer, Eiko Ishioka, in which the interrogation area is a large room dotted by ornate columns.

An even greater influence on "Chain of Command" was STAR TREK itself. It's genesis is in a story Ro Laren relat-

ed to Picard in "Ensign Ro", where she revealed that her father was tortured in front of her eyes and killed by Cardassians during the occupation of Bajor. Ron Moore was assigned Part One, having an instant affinity for the Jellico storyline, while former Supervising Producer Frank Abatemarco took on Part Two.

Abatemarco, who had yet to prove he could write STAR TREK, had his job riding on his teleplay for "Chain of Command" and he received copious notes from Jeri Taylor. Reportedly, Abatemarco was excited about the chance to delve into such a thorny subject and did intensive research, consulting Amnesty International about the torture of political prisoners.

"The show was a wonderful exploration of psychological torture," said Brannon Braga. "Frank did a lot research. A little research goes a long way. He may have done a little too much and his research was showing. There just comes a point where you have to step in as a writer and use your instincts as a person and a writer to bring to life these situations and step away from the research a little bit. I think that's why the first draft suffered. Obviously, Jeri came in and gave it the psychological depth and punch it needed."

Despite the fact that

Taylor did a page one rewrite on the teleplay, she does not receive a screen credit on the show, which has upset many of the staff members and happens all to frequently on television. Said Taylor of the initial Abatemarco draft, "I have been a member of Amnesty International for a number of years and have been supportive of their causes. Frank did tons of research. He worked with a group that are surviving torture victims. He talked with a psychiatrist who specializes in treating torture victims and did reams of reading. He did absolutely the most wonderfully exhaustive kind of research. So I was very comfortable that we were getting the best possible tack on it. Patrick called me after reading the first draft to say he was delighted to know that we were doing this and told me of his involvement with Amnesty International. I said, 'Great. I have to tell you that it's going to be rather substantially rewritten.' Patrick got very concerned because he assumed that meant we were going to back off from the very strong nature of it. He said, 'I don't want that to happen. I think that this hits it head on. I want to do that. I don't want this to become another talky episode where we simply talk about and around something and don't really tell it the way it is.'"

Stewart's concerns, however were shared by Taylor who just didn't feel the script was working yet. "I said, 'Patrick, please trust me. We won't do that, but I think that we can get more out of the script.' And he was very uncertain and disconcerted. He said, 'Well, I'll wait until I see the rewrite, but....' and then he got the rewrite and called back. He was thrilled because we didn't back off an inch. It was very strong stuff."

Stewart turned in a tour de force performance. In the episode, Picard finds himself unable to prevent being mentally and physically assaulted and, in one scene — during which the set was closed to almost everyone but absolutely essential crewmembers — stripped and cuffed to a rack.

"It's a very gutsy and nude performance," said Brannon Braga of Stewart's acting, which provoked some protest among viewers. Said Jeri Taylor, "They didn't want to see Patrick Stewart or anybody else writhing in pain. They felt that it was excessive, that it went too far and that it was disturbing to children. I can't disagree. It's certainly very intense for children. I wish there had been a disclaimer."

Due to the fact that many independent stations won't broadcast a disclaimer because advertisers will immediately pull out if a parental advisory warning is broadcast, the episode did not include a warning during the airing of the show. For Taylor, however, the show was not gratuitous in any way and exposed the twisted abuse of power that exists throughout the world today, touching on a very important and topical contemporary issue.

"I wouldn't even look at Frank's books," said Taylor. "This whole subject upsets me so much that I can't even listen to a news report about it. I didn't want to watch 'Closest Land.' Ultimately, I felt that it may be unpleasant to see an actor representing pain or pretending to be in agony, but we should all realize that there are tens of thousands of people in the world, every minute of the day, that are undergoing that kind of excruciating agony and that 80% of countries in the world routinely use torture. That is an important message to get across. People should be aware of that. We cannot hide and protect ourselves from it. If strong material might motivate people to get involved with an organization like Amnesty International, then it was well worth doing."

"She really brought a lot to those very difficult scenes," said Ron Moore. "It sounds great in a theater. You put two characters in a room and watch what happens. But we can also be dead if it's not handled right and Jeri displays a humanity, compassion and drive in the things she writes and she deserves a lot of credit for that show."

Added Taylor, "I responded personally to the people who wrote me to say that they were disturbed by the episode. I said that I understood that and suggested that they might find some expiation of those feelings if they contacted Amnesty International and became involved, because they could find that they could write letters on behalf of torture victims and turn those feelings of anxiety into something positive that might have an affect that would help someone else."

Unfortunately, in the money crunch, the resolution of the Cardassian space opera suffered with most of the action transpiring on the Enterprise's main viewing screen. Commented Ron Moore of the conclusion in which Jellico mines the Cardassians ship, "We just couldn't afford the big opticals of having the Enterprise facing off the against the fleet in the Nebula. By that point in the season, we had done a lot of expensive things. That show had to save us some cash. It had to be the money saving episode."

For Brannon Braga, the resolution of the conflict between Jellico and Riker proved unrewarding. "My only disappointment is that Riker didn't rise to the occasion more," he said. "I wanted to see Riker tell this guy to fuck off and make him step down and take charge of the situation and it never happened. There was a swell of conflict in the scene in Part II where Riker tells him off, but that's all he does is tell him off. I felt that we neutered Riker a little bit in that episode."

In Part II, Richard James needed to create an interrogation chamber for David Warner's Gul Madred, who tortures Picard. During early production meetings, "Closest Land," a movie in which Alan Rickman tortures Madeline Stowe, had been cited as an influence, but it was one that James avoided. "I wasn't familiar with it and I didn't want to be influenced by that because I was fighting SILENCE OF THE LAMBS at that time as well," said James. "I really wanted to try and keep myself open to my own kind of vision of it and as it turned out, the lighting played a very important role in what I was planning to do with it and the starkness of it. I wanted it to feel big as opposed to feeling like they were stuck in a small dungeon type thing."

"The original scripts were a lot more graphic," said Livingston of the two-part TREK torture piece. "We toned a lot of it down because it wasn't really germane to the story. The story is really about a struggle between the torturer and the torturee. The psychological thing that goes on even though the physical pain is excruciating. Patrick played it really well."

Episode #138
"Ship in a Bottle"

Written by Rene Echevarria
Directed by Alexander Singer

Guest Starring:
Daniel Davis (Moriarty), Dwight Schultz (Barclay), Clement Von Franckenstein (Gentleman), Stephanie Beacham (Countess), Majel Barrett (Computer Voice)

Sherlock Homes' archnemesis, Moriarty, created in second season's "Elementary, Dear Data," is accidentally released from computer stasis while Barclay is performing a holodeck diagnostic. The super-genius threatens to destroy the ship unless Picard finds a way for him and his computer-generated lover, the Countess Regina Barthlomew (SEAQUEST's Stephanie Beacham), to leave the holodeck. In the episode's coda, Picard offers dryly, "Who knows, our reality may be very much like theirs and all this may be an elaborate simulation running inside a little device."

••••

"I pitched a story after I sold 'The Offspring' about Riker and Picard going on a mission, and Riker beams him into the holodeck from Starbase and it appears as though Riker is taking over the ship and leading it into enemy territory," said Rene Echevarria. "In fact, what he's doing is setting up a scenario where Picard will be protected. It was a plan to discredit some bad guy and Michael remembered it and said he loved the holodeck gag. When we were all at Jeri's house one Sunday having a story session, somebody mentioned we could do Moriarty again. I told everybody there was a story Michael liked that we could use. In the first draft, we figured out a way to do help him escape the holodeck by walking in a transporter beam and it breaks up and he dies — but during the break we came up with the notion of giving him what he wants and never letting him know he's been fooled. It was very sweet, having this 18th century genius thinking he'd outsmarted us and just smugly going on."

"I had a peculiar affinity for the theme since I have worked on the holodeck of the 20th century, virtual reality,"
said director Alexander Singer. "I worked for MCA/Universal in developing it as a technology and I'm still involved. The most difficult aspect of the show was the casting, because the lady put a strange romantic hue on the whole piece. Her casting was the most difficult because we needed someone who could pull off an English accent and had a regal appearance, but who was also very sexy in Victorian clothes. When I saw Stephanie I said that's it, end of story.

"She's a very sexy, aggressive, direct and attractive person," added Singer of his leading lady. "The worst problem I had being the new boy in town is that I still make some interesting faux. The first one happened because of the Victorian dress that was required. Victorian clothes are probably, without exception, the ugliest styles that possibly the human race has ever put on a woman. And I was very concerned that the lady be a knockout."

Singer's concern that his leading lady be properly attired led him and his star to the wardrobe department, where they proceeded to wreak havoc in Bob Blackman's absence.

"She came in like a whirlwind and the two of us got involved with people in the wardrobe department. There was something they
had put together on a mannequin that looked all wrong and horrified her. My sense, as a director, was if you're leading lady is upset at wardrobe and is worried about it, you've got to solve that problem. What I saw on the mannequin was not going to do it. I joined her in what was a kind of devastating runthrough in the department with assistants to Blackman. The two of us left a trail of disorder and confusion that must have been, in retrospect, either ludicrous, or laughable or infuriating depending on who you were. The next day Mr. Blackman comes on the set, takes me off to the side, and says to me in more or less plain language, 'Do you know how many Emmys I've gotten for this show? Do you understand that I am a recognized expert in this area? I am not going to destroy your actress. Let me do my job. Suppose I came on this set and told you where to put the camera, you wouldn't particularly like it.' I said, 'I'd try to kill you' and he said now you know how I feel."

Singer, who realized his mistake, apologized, and was ultimately incredibly satisfied with the final result. "He told me what he was planning and reassured me and the next day when she appeared, I could not have imagined how good

••••

she looked. She was gorgeous and Daniel's performance was splendid and was up to doing anything that we had to do."

Said Brannon Braga, "My favorite kind of show, a twisty turny complex mystery. In this case I thought it worked pretty well and certainly the pairing of Moriarty and Barclay was inspired. This was such a good show, you had to do it. It's a great title. I tried to kick things off with 'Realm of Fear', which sounds like an old series. One of my favorites."

**Episode #139
"Aquiel"**

**Written by Brannon Braga &
Ron Moore
Story by Jeri Taylor
Directed by Cliff Bole**

Guest Starring:
Renee Jones (Aquiel), Wayne Grace (Governor Torak), Reg E. Cathey (Morag), Majel Barrett (Computer Voice)

Geordi falls for a presumably murdered woman while studying her journals in which the Klingons are suspect. But then the woman turns up alive, becoming the prime suspect in another gruesome killing aboard a subspace relay station.

• • • •

"We were looking for a new spin to put on a love story," said Jeri Taylor of the storyline inspired by Otto

Both the DC Comics and, finally, the live-action Next Generation *have decided to give Chief Engineer Geordi LaForge a love life (comic cover copyright © 1989 DC Comics).*

Preminger's LAURA at the suggestion of Michael Piller. "A straight love story didn't seem good enough. Geordi falling

in love with someone he thought was dead gave it just a nicer kind of feel. Of course, she seemed like an unobtain-

• • • •

able person or non-real, which we had seen before with his character, but it quickly turned around. The thing we all wanted to happen was to keep it open for a continuation of the relationship, since we would like to have one of our characters have an ongoing and committed relationship. After we lost the O'Briens, everybody in the 24th century is single and I think it might be nice to suggest enduring relationships are not going to be gone in the future."

"'Aquiel' was a torturous experience," recalled Brannon Braga. "We wrote it together which was fun, but Piller wasn't happy with the way it was going and he had some good story instincts. I thought it was going to be terrible, but when I sat down and watched it I kind of liked the mystery. I rather enjoyed that the dog did it. Ultimately, I didn't think the romance part worked but I liked the feel of the episode, which had a rather tragic, mysterious feel to it. Ultimately, disappointing because the romance didn't work. We wanted to do a Geordi show and one of the inspirations for this show was the movie LAURA with a science fiction twist. 'Aquiel' was a very fun and compelling process to break in the structure session. It was Jeri, Ron and I spending two days doing

it and if you could see that what we started out with and ended up with at the end of the break session was such a rich and interesting show. As a writer, sometimes because you're privy to all the development, you appreciate the show more. You appreciate the process. Whereas a viewer just has the show. It's interesting how the perceptions can be so different. I think the romantic relationship suffered. I never felt any chemistry between the two of them, something wasn't happening, maybe it was the writing. It's always a little contrived to get the actors together like this. All in all, I was more satisfied with the mystery and less satisfied with the romance. The Klingon story is the red herring and that's fun. The subspace relay station looked very cool. It was not classic TREK, and a lot of people hated it."

"I thought it was nice little runner," said Ron Moore of the subplot in which some disagreeable Klingons are accused of the murder at the Federation subspace relay station. "I didn't want to make that any bigger than it was. But in the final product, it was one of the more intriguing things. I never thought it would be, but it was just a cool little C story. Brannon and I wanted to name the show 'Murder, My Pet', but

cooler heads prevailed. In our first draft we really tried to get inside Geordi's head and give him all kinds of backstory and family history, but it was so loaded down with it that it didn't work. We had to go back and say, 'What's that love story again?' It's just when you combine a murder/mystery with a love story, you cheat it to some extent."

Episode #140
"Face of the Enemy"

Written by Naren Shankar
Story by Rene Echevarria
Directed by
Gabrielle Beaumont

Guest Starring:
Scott MacDonald (N'Vek), Carolyn Seymour (Toreth), Barry Lynch (DeSeve), Robertson Dean (Pilot), Dennis Cockrum (Alien Captain), Pamela Winslow (Ensign McKnight), Majel Barrett (Computer Voice)

Counselor Troi awakens aboard a Romulan warbird and finds she has been transformed into a Romulan officer, Major Rakal, a member of the feared Tal Shiar. She learns she is on a secret mission to assist in the defection of several important Romulan dignitaries to the Federation, bringing her into conflict with the captain of the Romulan ship, Toreth (Carolyn Seymour) — and the Enterprise.

....

Marina Sirtis and friend outside her trailer on the Paramount Pictures lot.

Naren Shankar's second writing assignment for the show was "Face of the Enemy", in which Troi finds herself playing 007 aboard a Romulan warbird. "I wrote the first draft of the script in six days because we were really under a time crunch. I was assigned it as a freelancer and halfway through I was brought on staff. The rewrite helped smooth out a lot of things and we had to change the ending a couple of times. The action in Act 5 didn't work initially. It was harrowing but it came out well. I think Marina Sirtis is a fine actress and when given the roles and characters to play, she does a terrific job and I was very happy with what she did. I would have been more than delighted to write other stuff for her. I go out of my way to look for stuff for Troi to do because I feel the character is underused."

Enthused Ron Moore, "Troi kicks some serious butt, which was nice."

"The show worked out very well," said Michael Piller. "There was trouble in getting THE ENEMY BELOW dynamic going at the end of the show and it suddenly just sort of fizzled out, but I thought it was a very successful episode. Marina is one of the great talents and nobody really knew it when this whole thing started. The more we give her to do,

the more she seems capable of doing. You do 'Man of the People' where one scene she's a sexpot and the next scene she's a crazy killer. In this show, she's fundamentally forced into being a secret agent. She has an extraordinary range."

"I thought 'Face of the Enemy' was great and I have to give myself a plug here that it was the top rated show of the season," said Sirtis. "Michael Dorn and I were having a competition because he thought 'Birthright' was going to win, and it didn't, and I was so happy. Troi as a Romulan is bizarre because she's so opposite to what a Romulan is."

Co-Executive Producer Jeri Taylor's desire to make this STAR TREK's "year of the woman" was reflected as well in "Face of the Enemy."

"I thought it was a great role for Marina," said Taylor. "I thought it was well written for her. I loved Carolyn Seymour as the Romulan Commander, she was outstanding in it. When those two women tee off against each other, it's great because we don't have that much conflict among our people, but between those two it's just spit and vinegar and they were dynamic. I enjoyed seeing those two powerful women get a chance to sort of rise to the occasion and take off on each other."

"Carolyn was great," agreed Sirtis. "We became firm friends. She was fabulous and I think I owe her a lot. I've seen that episode twice and I wasn't completely happy with my performance in it, but I thought a lot of the credit went to Carolyn, she was a great Romulan commander."

Naren Shankar, as a fan of the original show, is quick to note how it seems the characteristics of the Klingons and Romulans seem to have reversed in THE NEXT GENERATION, with the Romulans being cruel and barbaric and the Klingons obsessed with honor. "Their personalities flipped in the two series," said Shankar. "It's worked out well because the Romulans were not ever developed very well in the original series. In fact, the Romulans in 'The Enterprise Incident' are much more like our Romulans now than the Romulans in 'Balance of Terror', as they're holding people for questioning and torture."

"We were sitting around talking about this show and about who this important person would be that's defecting and Michael got this look on his face and said, 'We probably can't do this, but what if the person is Spock? They're getting out and at the end they open it up and it's *not* Spock. The person we take out is defrosted and we ask him what happened to Spock and he says, 'Spock didn't make it.' I look at Michael like he's crazy and he goes, 'Nah!'"

Shankar, a longtime TREK fan, even suggested casting Joanne Linville as the Romulan Commander as she starred in the original TREK's third season episode, "The Enterprise Incident. Lack of availability precluded this option. "The name Tal Shiar came from the episode 'Journey to Babel'," said Shankar. "I'm embarrassing myself by showing my TREK roots, but in that episode one of the Tellurite ambassadors is killed by a Vulcan execution method called Tal Shiar and I corrupted that and made that the name of the Romulan secret service. We have talked about bringing back Commander Toreth. She had enough ambiguity to keep it interesting. There are moment when she comes off sympathetic, but doesn't really care that the spaceship was blown up, only that it wasn't her order to fire. She's more than happy to kill people."

"We talked a lot about whether the character of the Romulan commander would be a man or a woman. We finally decided on a woman, but we had also talked about there being a little bit of a feel of HUNT FOR RED OCTOBER

in the show. When I was writing it I just had this strong image of Sean Connery, so all the dialogue I wrote for the show was with Sean Connery's voice in my mind, and then I just changed the name. The interesting thing is there's a line 'The Federation is neither stupid or foolish,' and I was going off like that. And then to see the same words — with not even a punctuation mark changed — played by a woman was a very interesting thing. It was the same exact words with a different delivery and a different attitude and it worked really well. It was the ultimate gender-blind writing."

Richard James was responsible for showing us the interior of the ship along with its quarters and command area. "We played off of Romulan having a motif represented by certain colors," he said. "We do that for identification so that certainly the Romulans would not have everything that would look just like Earth society. For us to graphically sell the idea of it being Romulan, we need to do it well with the sets, make-up and costumes which are Romulans colors. It helps to reinforce the idea that this is Romulan territory and it was not that much of a challenge because we played off of what's been established for Romulan ships."

In addition to the bridge, viewers saw for the first time a Romulan commissary, which couldn't be easily stocked with "Crate & Barrell" furnishings and utensils. "We had rooms that we'd never been into before for the Romulans and we said what would the Romulan plates and silverware look like?" mused James. "You get into all of that — and even simple things like chairs, which you had to design. It's not as though you could go out to the rental store. All these factors come into play."

Not everyone was necessarily pleased with the final result, including "Face of the Enemy" scripter Naren Shankar who had a different idea for what the warbird interiors would look like.

"What we ended up with was Romulan Pizza Kitchen," said Shankar. "If you read my first draft, I was very specific about what the Romulan bridge should look like. I thought we were going to build an entirely new set and the bridge I described was in an elongated room much like the nose of the Romulan ship. I wanted it to look alien and have the Commander standing at a rail in the back of the room. She always stands, there's no seat for her and the room ends with her back at the wall so there's no one behind her. The idea is they're so suspicious that the commander would never let anybody behind her. The entire cabin is forward of the command position and there's just one pilot and stations around that. To me that would have been cooler."

Episode #141
"Tapestry"

Written by Ronald D. Moore
Directed by Les Landau

Guest Starring:
John DeLancie (Q), Ned Vaughn (Corey), J.C. Brandy (Marta), Clint Carmichael (Nausicaan #1), Rae Norman (Penny), Clive Church (Maurice Picard), Marcus Nash (Young Picard), Majel Barrett (Computer Voice)

It's not such a wonderful life for Picard when Q (John DeLancie) gives him a chance to relive his rambunctious youth. As Picard lies dying in sickbay from a wound sustained on an Away Team mission, he finds himself in heaven with Q, who gives him a chance to stop the fight which led to the captain being fitted with an artificial heart.

••••

"I'm very proud of 'Tapestry'," reflected writer Ron Moore. "I liked it a lot. I immediately fastened onto the idea of Picard going into the white light and having a near death experience and there's

John DeLancie reprised his now famous role of "Q" in sixth season's "True Q" and "Tapestry" (photo copyright © 1993 Karen Witkowski).

Q. The problem is then what do you do? It was also my first shot at doing a Q show and I pictured the line, 'You're dead and I'm God,' as the first thing that came to mind as we started doing the episode."

Moore's first draft departed from the final script in many important respects. Entitled "A Q Carol", Q led Picard through pivotal scenes in his life much the way the ghosts of "A Christmas Carol" took Scrooge to the past, present and future. The irony was not lost on Moore who was of course cognizant of Stewart's recent star-turn on Broadway as Scrooge in "A Christmas Carol."

Said Moore, "Q took Picard back to several points in his life. The 'Samaritan Snare' story was one where he is attacked and needs to get

an artificial heart. There was a scene in France with him as a kid with his parents and I even considered doing the Stargazer and having Jack Crusher there."

The premise however was not only too expensive but failed to enthrall series Executive Producer Michael Piller. "He thought it was pointless," recalled Moore. "Here are some scenes from your life basically. It didn't have the right resonance so I went back and tried to focus in on one incident to make it a little more meaningful."

In the episode, Q gives Picard a chance to relive his youth where he helped a friend, Corey (Ned Vaughn), rig a gambling table to help get even with a Nausicaan who cheated him, and is almost killed in the ensuing fight.

••••

This time Q offers Picard the opportunity to avoid the conflict that led to him being stabbed through the heart, but rather than change his life in a positive way, Picard finds himself in the midst of disintegrating friendships, a failed love affair and, ultimately, an unfulfilling career when he is returned to the Enterprise as a junior grade lieutenant.

The story of Picard's uproarious youth and artificial heart was first revealed in "Samaritan Snare" and mentioned again in "Final Mission." In both cases, they involved Picard reluctantly confessing some of his youthful indiscretions to Wesley.

"It was an interesting little story about him," said Moore. "That story, to me, said a lot about Picard's character - that he was a different guy in those days. Then he changed. Why did he change? What would be the difference in the young womanizing, hard-drinking, hard-fighting Jean-Luc Picard and the guy that we know today?"

Moore's speculation had been informally discussed among the staff where they compared the evolution of Picard and another Enterprise captain, James T. Kirk, which in their view were completely opposite in terms of their personal development as characters. "In a way, he and Kirk went through life quite differently. Kirk in the Academy in those days was a bookworm; straightlaced, straight arrow and very uptight. You would call him a stack of books with legs — and then he became this wild man. He went out in the fleet and got comfortable and started doing all this crazy stuff. Picard went the other way. He was a wild man in his youth and then sort of became a little more mature and collected as he became an adult."

Said Story Editor Rene Echevarria of the episode's break session, "We sat down and came up with the idea that what he's dying of is the artificial heart. We talked about his heart failing and going back in some time to a part of his life, and then about the idea of it having to do with the incident that caused his heart to fail. We researched what had been established on screen and I think the payoff for the real fans is that in the original mention he says he laughed, which was a throwaway line. Finding a reason *why* he laughed in 'Tapestry' made for a wonderful moment. It made us all think we had really come up with the right story for the premise and tying that together. I think it's one of the finest efforts ever."

"I thought it was a terrific script," said John DeLancie, who returned to play Q in the story which may or may not have been a dream for Picard. "I thought that script was a pleasure to work on because it had such a straight throughline, you knew the direction you were moving in and you knew it from the beginning. I just thought it was terrific. There was a speech at the end where I talk about what he would have been and how dare he talk about what he might of been without being the type of man who would have taken the risks to get those things, which I thought was a tip-top speech. I just thought that show from beginning to end was terrific."

Opined Ron Moore, "I thought Patrick and John both did a great job. It's the best Q episode that they've done together. When Q is in the white limbo set, I thought the way he played that was so interesting because he played it real low key for Q. He was saying the lines but he was so low key about it that it added a lot of weight to it. It seemed very real because he wasn't just being goofy and running around and laughing. There was a sense that this is heavy shit."

That, however, was not the only reason DeLancie was low-key. One of the last scenes to be filmed for the episode was of Q and Picard in the afterlife, and in it Q wore a white robe. Filmed against a lit white background, Director of Photography Jonathan West and Producer Merri Howard were concerned that Q could become lost in the overexposed HEAVEN CAN WAIT imagery. Both actors were well aware of the difficulties involved in shooting the scene and feared that it may need to be reshot. The dailies were sent out for immediate development to ascertain whether Q would turn out to be nothing more than a floating head.

"Unfortunately, I think we were all a little bit dragged down and out in all those heaven scenes because of that," said DeLancie. "We started shooting it and it was already late and it was just getting later, and I think we all looked pretty tired."

When Picard returns to his Starfleet Academy days, he also encounters an old platonic girlfriend which this time around turns out to be less than platonic. Played by actress J.C. Brandy, Marta rebuffs Picard after they've slept together as Picard begins to watch his life unravel despite having the best of intentions. "The morning after scene was about four pages," said the actress. "I actually like it a lot better the way they cut it. I had this whole speech which I didn't feel was really me. It said the same thing that

J.C. Brandy portrayed Marta, Picard's former classmate and, thanks to Q, lover in "Tapestry".

the scene showed in one minute. Picard comes in and the beginning is the same, but I had this whole speech about how when we first met at the Academy and the Admiral said, 'Look to the left, look to the right of you, one of you isn't going to make it through the next four years and I thought that's me, I'm not going to make it and I looked to the right and there you were with this cocky look on your face which I thought was so great and I knew from that moment I wanted to be your friend.' The thing that bothered me about that line is to say something like I thought 'That's me,' is such a self-pitying thing to say. You have to be very careful while acting not to fall into that trap. No matter how you deliver it, that one sentence changes the character and that's why I was kind of glad they cut it."

Another concern of the young actress was her scenes with Patrick Stewart. "I was a little nervous," confessed Brandy. "I hate to stereotype anything, but you never know with British actors, especially because he's so good and so well trained. I felt a little intimidated going into it. Especially being a guest star. It's not that people are snobby to you, it's just that they do this every week, they're so set and they see people come and go and they don't have the energy to make an effort. Everyone, especially Patrick, made me feel immediately comfortable. Patrick was so nice and incredible to work with — and he likes Sondheim. I am completely in awe of his talent. He had one moment that just touched me so much — where you realize what a fine actor he is — when he first gets sent back in time after he gets slapped and leaves the room, and this smile comes over his face, it was just so beautiful. He's like watching a fine dancer."

Even more daunting for Brandy was bedding the British thespian who was more than twice her age. "It's very hard not to be taken in with Patrick," said the actress. "The way the end of the scene was written is she brushes her finger across his bottom lip and said something which basically fulfilled the male fantasy. We tried to play against that because I think if you get together with someone who's your best friend, there's a nervousness and innocence

which I thought was really captured in the scene which is why it worked, instead of playing the sex, Juliette Lewis-sucking-on-finger thing."

The age difference was not lost on Patrick Stewart, according to Brandy, who had her own anxieties when they were forced to redub the bedroom dialogue when the original sound recording proved unusable. "I think I made him nervous that I'm so young," she said. "Especially that first day he saw me. I think I really scared Les [Landau, the director] and Patrick when I came down to the set for my costume fitting, because I'm pretty low-maintenance and was wearing my overalls and had just stumbled out of bed and went down there. I looked around and met everybody and the next day I started work and they said we have to make you look as old as possible, because I look about 12 in my overalls."

The transformation included a typical STAR TREK make-over, which involved an elaborate hair-do and breast padding. "They did this glamour hair thing and I loved it, but the producers said this isn't what we wanted," she recalled. "'This isn't how she looked in the audition,' they said. Les had asked that they make me look as old as possible, and they didn't know how old I could look with make-up."

"It worked nicely, we downplayed the sex," added Brandy, whose mother turned bright-red when Picard kissed her. "The end was written so sexy, it was kind of a male fantasy thing. I think it worked nicely, I didn't think it was uncomfortable and it could have been because of the age difference. Unfortunately, we had to loop the whole bedroom sequence because the dolly was squeaking. Every single line in that was redone and that upset me. I was able to do it, but to me it took away so much from the performance. Of course, no one else is going to know the difference and what was amazing to me was that there was no difference in Patrick's performance. I was able to get the inflections and the rhythm right but there was a certain amount of intimacy in my voice that came from being very close to somebody instead of talking into a mike that I just wasn't able to get in the loop. It finally hit me why actors have nervous breakdowns, and if you let yourself get too upset about it it gets harder and harder."

Explained Rene Echevarria, "A couple of things were cut for time, including a one page monologue where she explains why this was the wrong thing to have happened between them and that it spoiled their relationship, and it was cut which was unfortunate. It was something that several of us had talked about: have you ever had a girl that was your friend and then one day it turns sexual and ruins the friendship? That was what the idea was and what the speech was about, and it had to be cut. We're hoping to see the two of them again."

However, the show — which many on the staff regard as the finest of the season — was received less warmly by some fans as well as Executive Producer Michael Piller. "I wasn't much a fan of that show," Piller stated. "I thought it was a wonderful premise, I loved the pitch of Picard dying and having the white light experience and reaching out to the hand and it's Q. It's your worst nightmare come true. I found that from the beginning my greatest fear was that it would be IT'S A WONDERFUL LIFE. When a series gets tired, they do IT'S A WONDERFUL LIFE. I don't think we ever solved my problems with it in terms of getting a fresh slant. I felt that it was one of those Christmas-type episodes where the direction and the performances were sort of flat. Some of the scenes seemed to be very talky to me, it did not have the power and the impact on me that it seems to have had on other people. I'm

As in this DC Comics annual, written by actor John DeLancie, Q decides to give Captain Picard the opportunity to alter his existence in "Tapestry" (comic cover copyright ©1990 DC Comics).

delighted that it was a meaningful experience for a lot of people and made them think about their own lives because ultimately that's what STAR TREK is trying to do. They should accept themselves rather than wish they had done something else."

However, not everyone appreciated that message. "We've gotten some flack about it," acknowledged Rene Echevarria. "People felt it glorified violence and that it basically says Picard tries to go back and not do the violent thing and solve things by reason and it makes him bland and not captain material. We got big, big letters from people saying this is awful and goes against everything STAR TREK stands for. I think the point the show made was much more subtle than that, and I think they lost sight of it."

Added Jeri Taylor, "The letters I've gotten make what I think is a valid point, which is that we seem to be coming down on the side of using violence to solve your problems. You get in a fight and you get stabbed and all of that and then your life turns out better. It was really disconcerting because that, of course, was not the intention. That wasn't even anything that entered our minds when we developed it. But standing back from it now, I have to say that I can see how people might see that that was sort of a message we were trying to communicate and it wasn't. And I now wish we had thought about how that might have come out. I'm

very anti-violence and so I would not want to think that we would be seen that way."

J.C. Brandy, a professed TREK fan, said of the coda in which Picard relays tales of his youth to his first officer, "That last scene gave me the chills. There was a lot more real human emotion there than is in most of the episodes I've seen."

"'Tapestry' was Michael's title," said Ron Moore. "We were talking about the story conceptually and what the message we were going to send was, and he just said you have to learn to set your part of the tapestry of your life and maybe that's your title. I thought it was a great title."

Moore suggested a shot for the conclusion during which Picard is regaling his first officer with tales of his youth. "I wanted an $11,000 shot which they made me cut," recalled Moore. "It would have cut to an angle outside the ops lounge seeing the two of them and the ship pulls away as they're talking, but it was so expensive. I kept fighting for that shot and I really wanted it, but finally we just couldn't afford to do it."

Recalled J.C. Brandy, "I read with the casting director and because of the nature of the episode I wasn't sure if it

was going to be Patrick playing himself or if they would have somebody younger," recalled J.C. Brandy. "I asked if it was going to be a QUANTUM LEAP kind of thing and they got a little testy and said, 'It's *not* going to be like QUANTUM LEAP.' After I got the part, all my friends were walking around like proud parents that I was going to be on STAR TREK."

Richard James was called upon to devise a bar which featured an alien game called Danjaq, which proved to be a pivotal element in the show's plot. "There were never any rules established," said James of the game. "It was a combination of a pool table and a pinball machine and I think we just play acted the game. There was never any logic to it. With the bar on that one, we treated it like a college hangout and it was dirty. We don't normally do too many dirty things. Our stuff is really pristine most of the time and all our crew doesn't sweat. That was not true of that bar. It was more down and dirty. We tried an institutional approach with the dorm rooms to get a little bit of the same feeling to it that we had with Starfleet Academy, which we felt it would probably be."

• • • •

Episode #142
"Birthright, Part I"

Written by Brannon Braga
Directed by Winrich Kolbe

Guest Starring:
Siddig El Fadil (Dr. Julian Bashir),
James Cromwell (Shrek), Cristine
Rose (Gi'ral), Jennifer Gatti (Ba'el),
Richard Herd (L'Kor)

On a visit to Deep Space Nine, Worf learns from an unscrupulous Uridian merchant, Shrek (James Cromwell), that his father may still be alive in a Romulan prison camp. At the same time, aboard the Enterprise, Data undergoes a power surge that causes him to experience a mysterious vision that turns out to be his first dream.

• • • •

"Certainly taking Data in this new direction is great," said Brannon Braga. "Without giving him emotions you're taking him in a very human direction, and I can't wait until next season when Data starts to have nightmares."

"We used DEEP SPACE NINE as a set," said Rick Berman of the first DS9/TNG crossover on the show. "I don't have a problem with that. I don't think it cross-promotes the show. It's fun for the fans and allows us to expand the STAR TREK universe in the NEXT GENERATION. Why not take advantage of it occasionally? I just don't believe in doing it for the sake of doing it. It's expensive and confusing when you have two shows up that you're trying to cross-produce."

Related director Winrich Kolbe, "Since I had worked on the show before, I was able to help the DP to come on the set before and tell him how we did it on DEEP SPACE NINE. It's a rather large set and it can strike terror in you when you sit and look at it and think that it could take three hours to light, but I knew where the prelights were and what was on and what was off. I was able to help Jonathan West in that respect."

"It was great doing THE NEXT GENERATION," said Siddig El Fadil, Dr. Julian Bashir of DEEP SPACE NINE. "It was at the end of the first half of the season on DS9 when the pressure was high. I was able to go on the NEXT GENERATION set where all these laid-back guys were, who had been doing it for years were hanging around. It was like taking some oxygen and then coming back to the set here where the pressure was on. The difference between making it important and it just being important naturally is huge, and here there was a pressure to make everything important. There they knew that if it wasn't good, you'd hear about it in no uncertain terms. So, make it good and have a good time at the same time. They did and that was nice. It was fun to work with them and they — Brent and LeVar — were both very fun."

"I cried," said Terry Farrell, who was originally supposed to appear in the crossover until scheduling conflicts forced Dax to be replaced by Bashir in the show. "I thought I should have fallen off the rock and disappeared in [DS9's] 'Move Along Home' instead of his character so I could have gone over there. I still have a couple of good scars on my knee from that one."

"It was a huge story," said Rene Echevarria of "Birthright". "We broke it as a one part episode and it took two acts of the script to get Worf down to the prison camp. The end of Act II was the what became the end of Part I. There was basically too much story to tell — and to do it justice, Michael said make it a two parter. He said you've got all this time on the planet surface so you'll be able to build a better compound and more sets and we came up with the Data story for Part One."

The story hadn't originally been considered for a two-parter, but when Michael Piller suggested it, the staff was more than pleased to oblige.

• • • •

"They had broken down the story on the board and I felt it was a really good one," said Piller. "Because this was season six, the season of taking risks, of not being afraid of doing things STAR TREK hadn't done before, I said 'Why not do another two parter? Why wait until the end of the season or wait for a Spock? If a story justifies being bigger than an hour, let's do it. I had been very happy with the results of 'Chain of Command' and I said to Rick we should do it and he said 'fine.' I also felt, much mistakenly as it turned out to be, that we would be able to save money if we expanded it into two hours by using the sets twice."

"It was one of my favorite shows," said Rick Berman of "Birthright I." "I loved every element of it and so did my son, Tommy, who's a very, very bright 11 year old, and it was his favorite episode ever. The B story and the A story were of equal importance to me, and it all clicked."

Once Piller had mandated that the episode become a two-parter, the challenge then became finding a B-story to fill out the first episode, which turned out to be the most intriguing plot development of the season: Data's dream.

"We were left with a problem, we needed another B

This model served as the initial conception for the compound that housed both Klingons and Romulans in "Birthright˜

story for Part I," said Brannon Braga who wrote the episode. "Ron [Moore] started talking about Data having a religious experience and then I had the idea what if he died and had a vision. We developed that idea and that break session was fun and went very smoothly. I really enjoyed writing the episode. I am compelled by dream imagery and surreal images, and this was finally a chance to do it on STAR TREK."

Said Rene Echevarria, "Brannon came up with the idea of Data flatlining and we were very concerned it was going to be to similar to 'Tapestry'. We started with the idea that it was a religious experience he had, but we quickly realized we would get ourselves into a lot of trouble

trying to say anything absolute or true about something so difficult to know. Instead we came up with the idea of Data dreaming, which I think worked really well. It was an unusual episode in that the two stories were very unconnected, but thematically they were."

In the episode, Data explains his vision to Worf and the Klingon urges him to seek out the true meaning of his dream and to find out whatever he can about his father. As he does, it dawns on him that he cannot ignore the possibility that his own father may be alive. Worf chooses to go to the Romulan prison camp where he has been told his father is still alive. "The scene where Worf tells Data about finding out the truth about the vision of your father is very powerful," said Echevarria. "It was one of the finest scenes in the history of STAR TREK. I thought it was lovely when Worf realized he was talking about himself and it tied the two stories together and sent Worf on his journey."

"The whole Data thing started in desperation and just saying, 'What can we do with Data? What haven't we done with Data?'" said Jeri Taylor of finding another storyline for the episode. "It came from the Klingons sort of having a mystical, mythical, spiritual side and we thought maybe Data can have one. It started originally as Data exploring a metaphysical aspect or spiritual side to himself. Does he have this? That just kept getting turned and turned until almost at the last minute where it became the dreaming thing, which Brannon then took and made this magical, wonderful, literally soaring kind of B-story that rightly took over the first part. To me, that whole story by itself is one of the best we've ever done."

Sugar seems to serve Brannon Braga well. It was while pouring syrup onto his pancakes one morning that he came up with the ending for last season's "Cause & Effect" and it was while eating birthday cake that he got his own vision for Data's dream.

"I said to Jeri what if he was deactivated and while he was shut down, he sees something, and it took off from there?" remembered Braga. "It was up to me to come up with the dream imagery and I really tried to delve into Jungian archetypes and dream images that had never really been shown before. At first Michael didn't find the Data dream story very compelling and he had a couple of notions to fix it, namely showing a piece of the dream early on, which I had not done. His suggestions were very good and made it work and in the end he told me he was very happy with the episode."

"As far as the character was concerned, 'Birthright' was the best concept for the character in a long time," said Brent Spiner. "It expanded an idea really nicely. I thought the idea of Data having a dream program was inspired and really excellent writing."

In visualizing Data's dream where the android encounters Dr. Soong forging a bird's wing on an anvil that turns real when immersed in water and flies away, director Winrich Kolbe was challenged with the task of providing the requisite surreal imagery required for the moments of Data's visions.

"I wanted to go all the way," said Kolbe. "I saw noth-

ing but shades of 2001. But it was decided by the powers that be, that we would not overexpose or underexpose. If we do anything, I was told we underexpose, but this is not what I had in mind. I wanted to actually flare it out to give it that different look, but some people felt that it had been done too often and would not look good. So then I decided I'm not going to talk about my creative input anymore, I'm just going to do what I want to do. I went over to [Director of Photography] Jonathan West and said, 'Now listen, what are we going to do? What can we do in here with a wide angle lens without going berserk?' And he said, 'A 10 mm is a perfect thing for this.' And so we ordered a 10 mm lens, which is a marvelous lens, and shot the whole dream sequence with that and a Steadicam."

"The bird gave a great performance," said Brannon Braga. "It's one of our best guest stars ever. Kolbe executed the dream sequences with finesse. I was very happy that everything came together for me on that episode. The two stories resonated thematically with one another and I don't have a single complaint."

"The big Romulan compound had all sorts of vegetation, but when we went on Christmas hiatus we had to strip all of that out of the stage and redo it," said Richard James of all the plants which had died from lack of sunlight during a break in filming in mid-December. "We had to pull the jungle and the vegetable garden out of the stage and redo all of that. It was a large set and we built the model for the matte shot and everybody took part in it and was done in a very short span of time."

Over the span of the two-part episode, Worf finds himself in many rooms in the complex including his personal quarters and in a large elaborate dining area. "We played the scene in the hall as a kind of all-purpose room and things went in and went out kind of like the great halls of a castle which were used for many different functions," said James of the redress of the complex's main set. "We approached it that way because we couldn't really build too much because we run out of space on the stages. We have a limitation of time, money and space."

In addition to the main prison complex, James also provided the forestry and lake where Worf first spots a Klingon, Ba'el (Jennifer Gatti) bathing. In shooting the massive set, director Winrich Kolbe pointed out he was influenced by former NEXT GEN director of photography,

Marvin Rush. "I learned to take the longest lens that you can get in there and keep whatever you want to keep in focus and let everything else fall out of focus. That way you don't see the hokieness of the sets. You gain some distance in there, and you stay away if things become more diffused. I'm very satisfied with what we did in the jungle. Jonathan [West] did a damn good job, because I wanted it to be night and I wanted it to be obscure. I didn't want to have harsh shadows or moonlight effect. I wanted to have an overall feeling that there was a light source, but I didn't want anybody to say 'What's up there? What's up there?' And he did that, and we came in shooting everything with 75 mm plus lenses, and I'm very satisfied with it. Even Michael Dorn, who was moaning and groaning because I did one shot where water drops on a leaf and then did a rack focus, thought that would be a little bit too much because we had never done it before. Once he saw it, he said, 'Hey, you know, it looks terrific.'"

Another problem the director encountered was shooting the Klingon compound when he discovered that one of the walls that needed to be reinforced for Worf to scale was, in fact, rather flimsily constructed. "On the last

day, we found out that the wall that was built a little bit sturdier for the stunt double and Michael Dorn to climb over was in the wrong spot," said Kolbe. "By that time it was too late to do anything, so we had to scramble at the last minute and start moving and getting him over the wall in one particular area and then bring him down in another area which had the reinforced wall, and then bring him back to the original area to make it appear as the proper continuity. I think it worked out to such a degree that nobody would notice unless he knew what happened. The set itself was very, very well designed. I had enough areas in there where I could put my camera in and get different angles, and that's the basic secret."

Kolbe also needed to shoot the nude bathing sequence in which Ba'el washes herself. "It seemed to me she was a little bit too dark. I should have lightened it up a little bit. The print that I saw was awfully dark. While shooting her, her breasts were taped and she wore a G-string, but still, in that distance, it's not what is actually happening in reality but what the audience perceives and they may have darkened the image to make sure that the audience didn't get the idea that, 'My God, our kids can't watch the show anymore because now we have nude women strutting through the jungle.'"

Said Echevarria, "It was a wonderful episode all the way around. Very well directed, the dream was spectacular. I'm only afraid 'Birthright Part II' was a disappointment."

Episode #143
"Birthright, Part II"

Written by Rene Echevarria
Directed by Dan Curry

Guest Starring:

James Cromwell (Shrek), Richard Herd (L'Kor), Jennifer Gatti (Ba'El), Sterling Macer (Toq), Christine Rose (Gi'Ral), Alan Scarfe (Tokath)

Worf attempts to instill a sense of heritage into the Klingons living in the Romulan prisoner-of-war camp while trying to execute an escape and rendezvous with Shrek (James Cromwell) to return to the Enterprise.

• • • •

Said Michael Piller, "I was the one who said instead of Worf being the human in the group, we've taken away so much of his Klingon Nature, let's give him back some and make him the gung-ho Klingon who says, 'You're Klingon, be true to who you are.' In a sense, I had just seen MALCOLM X and I said Worf is the guy who's saying 'You're black and you should be proud to be black.' That's where I started

from with the character standpoint, but when you get into it and you realize that there is something pretty good here and that he'll lose this woman he's in love with when he can't shake his own prejudice, it's a price he has to pay for his character and his code. I think that's great stuff. I think it's wonderful when people act in heroic ways that turn back on them. It's in THE MASTERPIECE SOCIETY as well. As long as you act true to your character and your own moral code and you think you're doing the right thing. It seems to be the right thing that ignorance is being bred there and these Klingons are being robbed of their traditions and own life."

Said Michael Piller, "The truth of the matter is that the best result of my decision to make it two parts I think did not turn out to be the Klingon story, but the extra story of Data's dream that was added to Part One. That resonated so nicely with the other wonderful, moving episode."

Michael Dorn, who plays Worf, enjoyed the episodes which provided continuing character development for the Klingon. "I thought it was great," said Dorn. "It also showed that this is like a bottomless well. It will never go dry. The Klingon story will just go on and on. We still don't

know if my father is really dead. Now that I have this girlfriend, she could even come back."

Executing the second episode was more difficult, requiring protracted discussions among the writing staff which were laced with philosophical differences and questions about Worf's actions in splintering the harmony of the contented prison camp inhabitants.

"I thought there was a wonderful BRIDGE OVER THE RIVER KWAI type story where you had a fundamentally charged relationship between a Romulan camp leader and Worf and this very interesting love affair where Worf had to reexamine his whole attitude towards the Romulans again," said Michael Piller. "It is always interesting to me whenever you can look at prejudice. I think the script turned out pretty well, the show just did not have quite the power I had hoped it would have. I don't really know why."

The episode was directed by Visual Effects Supervisor Dan Curry in his first directorial outing on the show. "I'm glad Dan did it because I've always liked him," said Michael Dorn. "He's a very interesting guy and very patient. We have a rapport and he was just wonderful to work for."

Curry, who had traveled

• • • •

abroad for many years, including in Thailand as a photographer before returning to America where he currently oversees all visual effects wok on THE NEXT GENERATION, made good use of his background for the show, utilizing photography from Laos in a matte painting of the compound which boasted a miniature built by the art department. "I invented the spear game using old spear throwing techniques from sword school in that," said Curry. "I've been doing second unit directing work on STAR TREK for five seasons and did live theater in graduate school as well as film. The best thing about this experience was the support from the cast and crew, particularly Jonathan West, our Director of Photography, who was a major collaborator and lifesaver. Everybody was looking out for me and the thing that gratified me the most was I implicitly trusted every member of the crew to do a great job and they did. Michael Dorn was really great. He couldn't have been a better person to work with. He delivered a knockout performance."

The show, which ran 12 minutes long, needed to be cut for time and as result several aspects of the story went sadly unexplained. The most conspicuous omission was the motivation of the Yridian, Jaglom Shrek (James Cromwell) who claimed that Worf's father, Mogh, was taken to the prison camp by the Romulans after the massacre at Khitomer.

"The first idea was cut for time from the script," said Rene Echevarria of Shrek. "One idea was that Worf was going to see he had some sort of tattoo of having been a prisoner and Shrek was going to talk about being a prisoner and that his government let him rot and it took his family to come and risk their lives to free him. He says he knows how governments can be and doesn't trust them. 'You think I do this for money, but I actually do it because I know what it's like,' Shrek tells Worf."

Another complication was that the actor who portrayed Shrek broke his leg between filming of the two episodes, severely curtailing his availability. "In Part II, the Enterprise was going to find Shrek and say where did you take Worf and he would stall and not want to tell us," said Echevarria. "Then a Klingon ship was going to come in and the Klingon commander demands to speak with Picard. The Klingon comes over to the ops lounge saying he has something to say about Shrek and says, 'He's a liar, he spreads lies about my family' and all of a sudden he just throws a dagger and kills Shrek. We wanted to show the other side of what was happening on the planet, which is that this Klingon would rather deny the possibility that his father might be a prisoner than what Worf did and show the reason that the Klingons who stayed did because of that reaction. Ultimately, it wasn't filmed. He waves to Worf and he's gone."

"The Yridian just kept getting diminished," said Jeri Taylor. "Rene had a wonderful notion that we take this guy who seems to be this grasping, inquisitive, sell-anything-for-a-buck-guy and what you find out in Part II is that he actually has some very strong motivations which was that he was a prisoner of war himself. We had several versions of that and some of it went because of time, some of it went because Rick felt it was almost manipulative to redeem this character who he thought was working effectively as a bad guy. Everything that we tried to say about him just kept getting whittled away. Finally there was just nothing left."

Shrek's development as a prison camp survivor can trace it's roots to the Hebrew word 'shrek', which means to scream, an intentional allusion made by Brannon Braga in naming the character. "And I named him Jaglom Shrek because I can't stand [filmmaker] Henry Jaglom. Shrek was conceived in the story plot development as a character who looks like a sleezeball that turns out to be very sympathetic. It was cut from 'Birthright I' and was non-existent in 'Birthright II' and now he comes across as one-dimensional. I felt it was an unfortunate loss."

As to whether Worf's father truly is still alive, Braga speculated, "In my mind I don't think Shrek really knew, I think he just knew Worf's father was at that battle and might still be alive. Some people think L'kor is Worf's dad and never really told Worf. I don't think that's true. I think the father thing was resolved in Part One when he finds out his father's dead and that's that."

Another scene that was cut from the final televised version was one between Ba'El's mother, Gi'Ral (Christine Rose) and Worf. "She takes Worf to task," said Echevarria, who wrote the teleplay for Part II. "She says, 'I was like you and the first year I was here, I was miserable and I cried,' and she talks about the son she left behind and will never see again and how she fell in love with Tokath and how she stopped seeing the hate and the pain. It was very nice."

Other cuts from the finished episode included some of Worf's stories of his Klingon heritage, which Ron Moore used in writing 'Rightful Heir.' Part II's ambitious storyline primarily revolved around Worf's attempts to instill in the children of the survivors of the Khitomer Massacre, who are prisoners at the camp, a sense of their Klingon heritage. "We were all so excited about it and it was a big, rich canvas of material," said Rene Echevarria, who wrote the teleplay. "I have the vague feeling I wasn't able to pull everything off." Among the other elements which suffered in the final cut were Worf's romance with Ba'El, the daughter of Romulan Prison Camp Commandant Tokath (Alan Scarfe) and Klingon Gi'Ral. "The love affair ended up being rushed," conceded Echevarria.

"I never liked it," concurred Naren Shankar. "I don't know if I was alone, but I've always had real difficulty with romance that develops in the course of one episode, even if time passages have been indicated. In retrospect, I think that was one of the strengths of 'Aquiel.' It's one of the few times I thought the romance was credible. We have a tendency to use Worf as our receptacle for all human frailty and prejudice, which is too bad because anytime we need a racist, it can't be a regular, so it's let's use Worf. Ultimately, that romance was so down-played in the episode I personally think you could have had the exact same effect without that romance there. Jeri would disagree with me. I see it as superfluous and conventional and unnecessary."

"I wanted more," admitted Brannon Braga. "I wished in Part Two they would have had sex, but they didn't. I wanted more of that and less philosophy."

Said Michael Dorn of his on-air tryst, "In the first draft this girl and I fell in love and there was nothing at stake in terms of the relationship. She all of the sudden showed up and I saw her bathing in a pool naked and we talked and all of the sudden she loves me and it's a big thing at the end that she leaves and I'm upset. Why would I be upset? There's nothing that happened. There has to be something at stake for you to feel bad about losing something. We had a nice compromise on that and sometimes it works, sometimes it doesn't, and I think this did."

As in the best episodes of STAR TREK, "Birthright" provoked controversy both in its hunting scenes and in its apparent sympathies with Worf's disruption of what some perceived as a utopian society. "It is a cultural thing and I think the difference between going out to the woods with a semi-automatic rifle and a spear is a world of difference," said Rene Echevarria of the mail they received regarding Worf's hunting scene with Toq (Sterling Macer). "In the natural world, most animals die in the jaws of another animal. You do not kill a thing unless you intend to eat it. It was a non-issue for me."

The other issue which aroused the ire of many viewers and evoked lively conversations on the staff revolved around Worf's decision to take the children away from the peaceful planet. "There was some faint concern that in general it was advocating violence," said Echevarria. "Worf comes in there and destroys a perfectly happy society. I think that's unfair. We worked very hard to make the Klingons and the Romulans likable — and perhaps we went too far. Ultimately, all Worf was saying is everyone has a right to choose where they want to live and what they want to do with their life and you're hiding the truth from these young people and they're not going to be able to do anything but sit in this camp for the rest of their lives."

"I felt the same way," said Michael Dorn. "I've always approached these things with a fan's eye, almost, looking at it skeptically, and how I would perceive it if I was just a fan of the show. It was

very interesting that Worf was that way because basically he knows Klingons are not the most honorable people in the world and they don't always do the right thing. The way it was explained to me was I called Jeri and said he's very intense about this thing and seems to be forgetting everything he's learned in the past. She said, 'That's true, but they've lost something. They don't know who they are and all Worf's trying to do is say, 'You can make your own decision about what you want to do, but know each society and the different part of your character.' It's like religion. When people are brought up in a two-religion family, the best thing you can do is teach them both religions and then let them decide. That's all we were doing. And I agree with that, I think that's the right choice."

Admitted Jeri Taylor, "I'm still sort of answering mail and fighting battles and defending us on that one. People feel that we took a society in which prejudice and hatred had been put aside and ripped it asunder, with Worf coming in and saying, 'No, I know better. I'm going to show you a better way,' and took all the young people away. And that's true, he did. I feel that Worf is one of our more interesting characters because he is flawed. He is who he is. He's

not a human. He's a Klingon and he is, after all, the person who let a Romulan die rather than give him a blood transfusion. He tends to be narrow-minded. He tends to be stubborn. He tends to be racist. You know, he is endowed with traits that arise naturally from his Klingon-self, and that's what those people are. It was not necessarily an heroic act, but it was an act that I think is very true to Worf's character and it addressed something that I had been thinking about for a while. I remember a very poignant letter from a native American who spoke eloquently about the value of preserving individual cultures, saying that there is a danger in assimilation in losing that sense of tradition and antiquity and history that had defined what a people are and given a secure sense of how they fit into the world. And when those things tend to dissipate, something very important is lost. To me, what that episode was about was Worf sensing that in himself and sharing that gift with others."

Said Brannon Braga, "I have philosophical uncertainties about what ultimately it's saying and I don't think it's saying anything very good. It's certainly an entertaining episode, but there was a great schism between Jeri and Rene and Ron and Naren about where the show should go. Somewhere along the line, we lost a little bit of perspective. The show was well done, it was well-acted and well-written. At the same time, I thought Worf came into this, from all appearances, utopian culture that represents everything STAR TREK is about and destroys it because of heritage. The appropriate STAR TREK thing to do would have been for Worf to present the option to the young people and say, 'Here's what you're about, you decide and if you would like to join me, we will go,' but of course his life was at stake which probably compelled him to take more extreme action than was necessary — but in the end he rekindled racist attitudes and advocations of violence within these young people and I think I took objection to that."

Despite an outcry that Worf be redeemed for his actions, including from her own husband, Jeri Taylor stands firmly by the episode's resolution. "People have said you should redeem Worf," she commented. "And I've said 'No, we're not going to redeem Worf.' He doesn't need to be redeemed. We didn't when he let the Romulan die. He's done nothing within the context of his own culture that's wrong. I don't want to do anything

which seems to apologize and say, 'Oh, we made a mistake there, so okay, now we're going to make it better by giving you a happy ending.' I don't think that's the right thing to do."

**Episode #144
"Starship Mine"**

**Written by Morgan Gendel
Directed by Cliff Bole**

Guest Starring:
Marie Marshall (Kelsey), David Spielberg (Hutchinson), Tim Russ (Davor), Tom Nibley (Neil), Alan Altshuld (Pomet), Tim de Zarn (Satler), Arlee Reed (Waiter), Glenn Morshower (Orton)

During a routine bayron particle elimination sweep of the Enterprise, terrorists attempt to steal trilithium from the ship's engines. Picard, the sole remaining crewmember aboard the starship, attempts to stop them from escaping with the deadly compound by pretending to be the ship's barber, Mr. Mott.

••••

"It didn't feel like STAR TREK to me," said Michael Piller of a show in which Picard grapples with women in Ten Forward, shoots another man with a crossbow and pulls the plug on a container that destroys an entire ship. "I liked the show and thought it was very effective and well directed by Cliff, but I was worried that

it was very violent, which troubled me. Picard slugging it out with the two women wasn't silly, and Patrick did his usual fine job, but it was derivative."

"This was a classic example of a bravura role for Picard," countered Executive Producer Rick Berman. "It had a real tone and style to the look of the show and I think Cliff Bole did a nice job directing it. I enjoyed seeing Patrick as an actor being able to get physical."

Patrick Stewart agreed, "I enjoyed the episode enormously. It's now in my top half a dozen episodes. It was wonderful to be out of uniform for an entire episode and to be on the ship without any of the other boring crew members."

"The hallmark of Michael's tenure on the show has been character, but once we did that, there's also room to do stuff that is just straight run and jump," says uncredited writer Ron Moore. "I think there's a recognition that sometimes it's okay to do an action show and not to have to try and strain the force of a character piece on top of that. It was fun to do a straight action piece and to just do comedy on the planet. What you rapidly ran into were the money considerations, as is usual with everything else on the show, so I had to pare back the run and jump and then

David Spielberg provided tremendous comic relief as Admiral "Call me Hutch" Hutchinson in "Starship Mine" (photo © NBC)

what we had to deal with is is this too brutal and too much killing? I'm always the one who kills people in script left and right, and people are always asking me top pull it back — it's not STAR TREK, and I'm always kill more, kill more!"

"'Starship Mine' went through a major restructuring at the last minute," said direc-tor Cliff Bole. "Michael Piller and Rick just didn't like the way it was going and they said page one rewrite. Pages were coming in about ten a day *while* I was shooting."

In addition to fending with the script changes, direc-tor Bole found himself working on familiar sets with new com-plications. Since the Enter-prise was in dock for its bay-ron particle elimination sweep, most of the vessel's systems were shut down, including the lighting, which led to Bole being forced to eschew the time-saving pre-lighting and work with Jonathan West to create new lighting schemes for every set.

"This was the first time I was able to shoot the starship in a down mode, color-wise, light-wise, and everything else," said Bole. "It wasn't as bright and up as you normally see it so it was a challenge. That was the first time that the sets have been shot like that. After six years, you can usually come in and say, 'Okay, we're going to key from here and we're going to do this and we'll do that', especially on the bridge, which is our phone booth, basically. That's where we go in and try to pick up some time to just change the concept of the lighting in the hallways and everything else. You normally come in and you hit the hallway lights and you pretty much have your fill. But when they're not there, you're starting from scratch."

Bole also lost a day of shooting when the schedule was truncated to a seven day shoot from an eight day for the ambitious shoot. The director feels it suffered as a result. "I had to cook," he said. "When you lose another 12 hours of production, it hurts creatively.

• • • •

The show still stands, but I could have added a lot more and so could the cameraman. At the end, the little thing he pulled out of the canister in Ten Forward, which was kind of like a grenade pin, you couldn't see. You didn't know what he had in his hands so we just didn't sell it. I should have - I should have done a little bit more."

Episode #145
"Lessons"

Written by Ronald Wilkerson & Jean Louise Matthias
Directed by Robert Wiemer

Guest Starring:
Wendy Hughes (Nella Daren)

Picard becomes romantically involved with the new chief of the Stellar Sciences department, Nella Daren (Wendy Hughes), who shares a mutual love of music. The captain confides in Nella his fifth season "Inner Light" experience, and is forced to send his paramour on a deadly mission to evacuate a Federation colony threatened by a menacing firewall.

• • • •

"My feeling from the start of that episode was you started off with a concept that was flawed," noted Brannon Braga of the Picard romance tagline. "We said let's do a Picard romance and then came up with this story, which to me

Wendy Hughes, most recently a co-star of Barry Levinson's Homicide, *fell in love with Picard in "Lessons".*

was somewhat hackneyed. With a show like 'The Host', we started off with a great science-fiction gag and said this would make an interesting love story. If you had started with 'let's do a Beverly love story', what is the chance you would have come up with that? It's a good way to start but you're going to do a show like 'Lessons' which does not have a very compelling science-fiction component. Ultimately, Rene did a great job on the script. There's something

about Rene's writing that's very touching. He always finds the genuine emotion."

Said Echevarria, "It's very off format. We cast a woman who's closer to Picard's age than the women we've seen him with in the past, like Jennifer Hetrick and Michelle Phillips, and we're all very happy about it. We wanted somebody who had weight as opposed to it being just purely sexual. It has to do with music and she's a musician and there's that initial bond.

• • • •

'Lessons' also deals with those issues of how difficult it is to go out with someone you work with, especially someone who is your underling."

"We started thinking about this last spring when we were brainstorming ideas and Michael said maybe it would be interesting to do a love story in which Picard is attracted to someone who is serving under his command," recalled Jeri Taylor. "I said 'Yes' and just sort of dropped it at that point. As the season wore on, we got to the point where any glimmer of a story that Michael already has an interest in becomes appealing. If you don't have any stories, you say, 'What was that idea about a love story, great idea — looking better all the time.' I gave the idea to some freelance writers, Jean Matthias and Ronald Wilkerson, who had never gotten to write a teleplay, largely because of time constraints, and they wrote the story and I thought this is never going to go anyplace. I gave it to Michael and he said, 'Great, let's proceed.' It seemed sort of ordinary to me and then they wrote the screenplay which was quite good and Rene took it over and added some very nice things to it. It had an honesty and simplicity to it that was very engaging. Wendy Hughes, who is a wonderful

actress, made the whole relationship believable. You believed that Picard would be enchanted with this woman and I was wrong from my lukewarm response to it at the beginning. It turned into something that was sweet and endearing."

"It's sort of a BRIEF ENCOUNTER on the starship Enterprise, and I thought that Wendy Hughes was perfect casting," said Michael Piller. "You really had to have that magic to make things work. It was a low-key ending, which may not be what you expect, but I thought it worked well rather than the potential handwringing."

Episode #146
"The Chase"

Teleplay by Joe Menosky
Story by Ronald D. Moore
and Joe Menosky
Directed by Jonathan Frakes

Guest Starring:
John Cothran, Jr. (Nu'Daq), Norman Lloyd (Professor Galen), Ken Thorley (Mott), Linda Thorson (Gul Ocett), Salome Jens (Humanoid), Maurice Roeves (Romulan Captain), Majel Barrett (Computer Voice)

When Professor Galen (Norman Lloyd), Picard's mentor, is killed, the captain pursues a trail of DNA fragments which leads the Enterprise to a planet which has already attracted feuding Cardassians,

Klingons and Romulans, all in a search for the secret encoded within the DNA fragment.

. . . .

Missing from the final cut is a scene that Ron Moore had written when it originally appeared the episode would running short, in which Mr. Mott (Ken Thorley) is approached by Dr. Crusher as one of the non-Federation aliens whose DNA may hold clues to the mystery. "I'm sure I've got the answer," he assures her. "What's the question?" Needless to say, Mott is dumbfounded when he finds out he's been of no use and insists that it's Beverly who's at fault. The scene ended up being cut when the episode ran long.

Said Rick Berman of "The Chase", "It's a story that's been around forever. It was similar to 'Darmok', which was a story that was around forever also. 'Darmok' never worked for me until Joe [Menosky] came up with the direction that he came up with — and it turned out to be one of my favorite episodes of all time. This story did not. Conceptually, it's very interesting. I always had some problems with dealing with the whole idea of these kind of prehistoric creatures who are the fathers of us all. It's not Roddenberry-esque, it's very '60s Roddenberry-esque."

"It's been a very tough

In "The Chase", Norman Lloyd portrayed Picard's mentor, Professor Galen, who sets the captain off on the adventure of his life.

concept to wrestle to the ground," said Michael Piller. "The script was a nightmare. Joe wrote a wonderful first 20 pages and then you turn the page and it begins to go into the tech. One of the great talents of Menosky has always been his ability to see places the rest of us wouldn't even go to look and from page 20 to page 60 he was on a different plane, existing somewhere else. I just had to keep feeding back material saying I don't get it."

Said co-writer Ron Moore, "Michael had a problem with the story early and that there wasn't enough character. He felt there wasn't a strong Picard drive for why he would do this, so it really means going and finding something about Picard to carry it through the episode. 'The Chase' was something that Joe and I had been working on for a long time in development. We knew it was going to be expensive and it took a long time to get it to the point where they wanted to do it finally. It's one of the things about television, you can decide how life began with the stroke of the pen and you

decide these kinds of issues."

"It's the most Roddenberry-esque show we have done," agreed science advisor/story editor Naren Shankar. "I think the original conception of this was a little bit along the lines of its IT'S A MAD, MAD, MAD, MAD WORLD, but it got more serious and I think that helped it. When we intend do comedy, we tend to do it rather poorly."

Offered Jonathan Frakes, "The speech that Salome Jens makes at the end would make Roddenberry very proud I think. It's a great cast and it's wonderful to have all those villains and aliens in one place. Linda Thorson played the first female Cardassian we have had and she was astounding. John Cothran, Jr., our Klingon out of Chicago, did a great job and was appalled at the idea that Klingons and Romulans and Cardassians could be vaguely related, which is what the last speech suggests. Norman, who was a wonderful actor and is a wonderful man, was terrific and, of course, this guy Maurice Roeves, who's like Tony Hopkins, was sensational, so we were very lucky with that cast."

"I was very disappointed not to get shoot outside," added Frakes. "I think it does look like Planet Hell, but that's the way it goes. The money's being spent across the street. I don't think its a secret."

Richard James disagreed, noting that it would have been impossible to use a location for the show because of story considerations. "We were actually going to do location and we scouted location and there was vegetation which we couldn't use. The location really needed to be the salt flats where there's absolutely no vegetation so we were really forced to do it on stage."

Episode #147
"Frame of Mind"

Written by Brannon Braga
Directed by James Conway

Guest Starring:
Andrew Prine (Administrator), Susanna Thompson (Inmate), Gary Werntz (Mavek), Allan Dean Moore (Wounded Crewmember), David Selburg (Doctor Syrus)

Riker finds himself propelled between life aboard the Enterprise and as an inmate of an alien mental asylum while acting for Dr. Crusher in a play, "Frame of Mind." Unable to discern reality from fantasy, Riker believes he really is insane and that the Enterprise is a figment of his imagination. Eventually it's revealed that he has been captured on an Away Team mission and the mind probe is actually an attempt to extract information from the commander.

Will Riker questions his sanity in "Frame of Mind". This shot of a considerably calmer Jonathan Frakes was taken at a recent convention (photo copyright © 1993 Karen Witkowski)

• • • •

Said Jonathan Frakes, who gives one of his strongest performances in the show, "'Frame of Mind' was really dark. It was a terrifying show and was creepy to do. [Director Jim] Conway came back and it was as big a show as I've had to carry. I thought he was very competent at the helm. It was wonderfully dark and I thank Mr. Braga for that."

"I had a notion: What if Riker woke up in an alien insane asylum and had no idea how he got there and was told he was crazy?" said Braga. "It was a very difficult show to structure, it took a long time.

• • • •

But ultimately, it became the most intricate structure of the season and Jim Conway did a brilliant job directing. Writing it was a challenge, but it utilizes a great deal of surreal imagery and eerie elements, namely Riker doubting his sanity which appeals to me a lot. It was fun for me to do. One of my favorite films is Roman Polanski's REPULSION, and I think the influence will show through. I've always wanted to write something about someone doubting their sense of reality and I think it works."

Added Naren Shankar, "I think this is the best script Brannon has ever written for the series. It was a phenomenally cool first draft and it's an incredibly great episode. It's a darker season this year which is funny because, in general, we're not a very dark bunch. Dark stories are very attractive, they're interesting and the emotions they bring up are attractive because they're powerful and off-putting. We have had some very intense episodes and gut-wrenching stuff. There's not a lot of light moments in 'Face of the Enemy' and 'Chain of Command.'"

Episode #148
"Suspicions"

**Written by Joe Menosky &
Naren Shankar
Directed by Cliff Bole**

Guest Starring:
Whoopi Goldberg (Guinan), Patti Yasutake (Ogawa), Tricia O'Neil (Kurak), Peter Slutsker (Dr. Reyga), James Horan (Jo'Bril), John S. Ragin (Dr. Christopher), Joan Stuart Morris (T'Pan)

Beverly is relieved of duty after investigating what she believes is the murder of a Ferengi scientist who has created a metaphasic shield designed to take a shuttle through a star's corona. Relaying the story in flashback to Guinan, Dr. Crusher is intent on solving the murder and salvaging her career.

••••

Said Rick Berman, "My biggest problem with this was it broke rules more than anything else this season. The teaser and the first three acts of this are done in flashback and narrated by Beverly. It took me a while to sign off on that. But everybody was very big on it and I think it worked out okay. STAR TREK is a narrated show in that it uses the concept of the log, I think it's dangerous to take that and expand upon it. We make it very clear to the writers that the captain's logs cannot be narration. They are basically a narrative tool that we can use to get from A to B but we don't use them to narrate the action that is presently going on. We're very careful in constructing logs and you never have a situation where Picard is in a sense telling us

what we're seeing. He's usually telling us what has happened prior to what we're seeing. There's a big difference. I think the logs are quite unique to STAR TREK and it's a great way to have Picard's voiceover be effective. Having a Tom Selleck-like narration [as in MAGNUM p.i.] is something we try to stay away from."

"I had a Ferengi in there that I had to reshoot because I let him get out of character," said Cliff Bole of filming the episode highlighting Gates McFadden as Beverly, an actress with whom he admits he has "butted heads" with in past. "He was a scientist, so I said that means he's got a little more compassion, maybe he's not as oily as the rest of them. I think I went too far and the guys asked me to reshoot a couple of scenes. Rick Berman said, 'Don't forget, they're still Ferengis.'"

"What I really wanted was a vehicle for Beverly," offered Jeri Taylor. "I felt we had given Troi some really nice things to do, Beverly has had more to do within a number of episodes but she did not have one that was all hers. We wanted to give her something atypical and not a female role. The idea of her playing a Private Eye or Quincy was very appealing. I don't know how successful it is. We had one whole story on it done and

Michael felt, rightly, that it was a nicely crafted mystery, but so what? We tried to find an angle that would give it a nice little spin. Who's the last person you would suspect? The person who was killed first. She takes on the world and gets in deeper and deeper because, of all things, she felt compassion for a Ferengi. She bucks the stream and goes up against Picard and disobeys an order. We had an unusual stylistic flavor that's offbeat."

Episode #149
"Rightful Heir"

Story by James E. Brooks
Teleplay by Ronald D. Moore
Directed by Winrich Kolbe

Guest Starring:
Alan Oppenheimer (Koroth), Robert O'Reilly (Gowron), Norman Snow (Torin), Charles Esten (Divok), Kevin Conway (Kahless)

While undergoing a spiritual crisis, Worf visits a Klingon monestary on Boreth, where the image of the legendary Klingon warrior, Kahless (Kevin Conway), appears to him. It is Kahless' intention to reclaim his position as leader of the Klingon Empire. Gowron (Robert O'Reilly), leader of the High Council, doubts the veracity of the ressurected prophet/messiah and challenges him in battle, leading Worf to the conclusion that Kahless is a clone.

Kevin Conway, the actor who portrayed the Klingon spiritual leader Kahless in "Rightful Heir"

• • • •

Interestingly, although much of the lore of Kahless is taken from dialogue that was cut from "Birthright II," Kahless actually first appeared in the original STAR TREK's third season episode, "The Savage Curtain." Played by actor Robert Herron, Kahless was considerably less friendly, representing one of the most evil people in galactic history.

"It was a difficult show

to do," said director Winrich Kolbe. "It started out rather conventionally, but once we got on Stage 16, we spent three days there. It was totally smoked in, in order to get that haze...I'm still coughing. The special effects people kept telling us it's non-poisonous and just a slight irritant. Well, I had a very heavy allergy which I think was caused by the smoke, but the show just look terrific. It looks a movie."

Of Michael Dorn's strong performance in the episode, Kolbe commented, "Michael and I have an interesting relationship. I try to push him and sometimes I push too hard and then he will fight back. Michael has matured since I met him four or five years ago. He has become a lot more secure and has become a lot better. That obviously helped on this particular show. He knew it was his show and we went in there from the beginning saying that we're going to make this the best show of the season — we might have a chance."

Added Michael Dorn, "It was a well written script. Usually you get ten different colors or changes, but in 'Rightful Heir' maybe there were two miniscule changes. Rick [Kolbe] and I had mini-discussions about where the character should be. He's wonderful and I trust him — so

if he says, 'Michael, try it like this,' you go, 'Okay' and you trust him. There are only one or two times where I said I don't agree, I think it should be another way. What he does then is he says, 'Let's try it both ways and we'll decide.'"

"It's a show which has some powerful metaphors for modern day religious beliefs STAR TREK has never tackled religion with such vigor as in this episode," said Brannon Braga. "The man playing Kahless as the Jesus Christ of the Klingon Empire was great and Michael Dorn's performance is powerful. It has the potential to be a very controversial episode that will take Worf's character in some interesting new directions."

Said writer Ron Moore of the episode, "This is a show I wanted to do. I thought it was a real nifty idea and I thought it was an opportunity to do a show unlike others we've done. The subject wasn't something that we tackled, so I was eager to do it. I wanted to do something interesting. I'm very proud of the script. It deals with faith and belief that we don't normally deal with on STAR TREK."

Countered Rick Berman, "I had a lot of fights with Ron about this. The character of Kahless and the backstory and the dialogue of Kahless were all a little bit too

on the nose Christ-like for me. We had a lot of long debates and eventually it was modified by Ron in a way that I think made it much better. I think he not only solved my problems but made the movie better. Kevin Conway's performance is great and it's a wonderful episode."

For "Rightful Heir", Richard James constructed a Klingon temple where Worf begins his spiritual quest for K'helest. "He did some great coverage on that set," said James of director Winrich Kolbe. "There's one long lense shot that makes the shot look like it goes on forever. It looks wonderful."

Episode #150
"Second Chances"

**Story by Michael A. Medlock
Teleplay by Rene Echevarria
Directed by LeVar Burton**

Guest Starring:

Dr. Mae Jemison (Ensign Palmer)

LeVar Burton's freshman directorial outing features Jonathan Frakes in two roles, that of Commander Riker and Lieutenant Riker, a duplicate created in a freak transporter accident eight years earlier. Still in love with Troi, Lieutenant Riker hopes to rekindle their relationship, while a fuming Commander Riker finds himself coming into conflict with his eager and abrasive dopelganger.

• • • •

"It was just a delight for me to write," said Rene Echevarria. "It was full of pitfalls but the first draft I turned in got the best reaction of anything I've ever done on the show. I made a lot of choices about how and why Troi and Riker broke up and people seemed to swallow them. It's another big Troi show and it's very romantic. We finally see Jonathan and Marina together kissing and it's just a wonderful romance."

"The most often asked convention question is what's happening to Troi and Riker," said Marina Sirtis. "We've never done a convention where that hasn't been asked in the first few minutes, and it's very difficult to tell them. 'Second Chances' I think shows where the relationship is now as far as the two people in it are concerned. Obviously Troi would resume it immediately if Riker opened that little door a chink — and Riker appears to have definitely closed the door on that relationship. That was an interesting kind of development. Because of the second Riker, we managed to actually see that Troi really does still love Will. Jonathan and I have this little running gag that they made a mistake and did the

wrong spin-off with DEEP SPACE NINE. The spinoff should have been 'The Rikers in Space', and now that we've met Lt. Riker there is a possibility that we will have the Rikers in space."

Said Brannon Braga of the episode, "I really like Riker and I enjoyed breaking this with Jeri and Rene. I was very moved, as is common with Rene's scripts. My theory is a TV show is in trouble when they do an evil twin episode and one could construe this as an evil twin if they hadn't already done it with 'Allegiance'. But this is not an evil twin, it's a tortured twin and it's a twin story I can buy. The main thing I contributed to Rene's brilliant script was the notion of the treasure hunt where Riker takes Troi on a romantic little treasure hunt of notes and gifts — which is a gag I have used in the past in my own romantic relationships to great effect. When all else fails, try the treasure hunt. It worked with Troi."

Reflecting the riskier nature of sixth season was that serious consideration was given to killing off Commander Riker at the end of the episode and allowing his duplicate, Lieutenant Riker, to come aboard as a new officer, completely reshuffling the Enterprise command hierarchy. It was a controversial consider-

ation, ultimately rejected.

"They seemed to be more concerned about it than I was," said Jonathan Frakes. "I figured as long as there was still a bearded officer on the ship, I would still have a job. I've had a couple of great shows. They've been very exciting and challenging and exhausting. They had talked about killing Commander Riker off and letting Lieutenant Riker live and then they were going to kill Lieutenant Riker off and they decided against both and sent Lieutenant Riker off to the Academy."

"It was fraught with controversy and problems and my heart tells me if I was an audience member, I would have been freaked out had they killed off my favorite character," said Brannon Braga. "The argument was it would infuse new life into the character, but it would have been a different character. If you're trying to sell that he's a different guy, which is one of the tenets of the episode, then you have to be prepared to say he's a different guy henchforth. I would have been angry, but my impulse is with the others, what a surprise, what a shocker, what a great season ender — but it wasn't done so it's a moot point."

Commented staff writer Naren Shankar, "The interesting speculation in 'Second

Chances' would be about the ending that we could have had. I was initially really against killing Riker and the more I thought about it, the more I liked it. It's really a super-unexpected place to go. The problem that I saw with it was we ran the risk of implicitly invalidating every choice that Riker had made his entire life for the last six years. You wouldn't even have to come out and say that, just the simple fact that the character is gone at the beginning of the episode. While it would have been really cool to have a Lieutenant Riker and Data as the first officer and have the new Riker struggling as the hothead, cockier Riker of his youth, the risk you run is you disassociate the character from his past, which is the only past the audience knows. While it's fascinating to think about in theory, I think ultimately we would have run into significant problems because it would have been impossible to play the kind of scenes with the texture we're used to between the characters. You're looking at a different flavor. I think probably it was the right decision, but it was very enticing. Suddenly, you energize that character in a whole new way. It's got some real selling points, but Michael and Rick said, 'No way. What kind of drugs are you taking?'"

**Episode #151
"Timescape"**

**Written by Brannon Braga
Directed by Adam Nimoy**

Guest Starring:
Michael Bofshever (Romulan/Alien)

Returning to the Enterprise via Runabout, Picard, Geordi, Troi and Data find the Enterprise apparently trapped in time in mid-battle with a Romulan warbird due to a strange temporal distortion. Leading an investigation aboard the ships in stasis, Picard realizes they must reverse time if they have any hope of saving the Enterprise and Dr. Crusher, who has been wounded by a phaser blast.

• • • •

Adam Nimoy returned to helm his second episode with "Timescape," a show which made "Rascals" pale in comparison in terms of technical complexity. While "Rascals'" physical challenges were easily apparent, "Timescape" presented a whole new range of problems for the director.

"It was absolutely bizarre," said Jeri Taylor. "It's full of opticals and complicated sequences. Do you do split screen? Do you do blue screen? Do you do anthromorphic lenses? It's endlessly complicated and here's Adam Nimoy back who got 'Rascals' first and now walks into this complicated directorial mess, and was very much on top of it. He's tremendously bright."

Said Rick Berman of Nimoy, "My feeling was that nobody should be asked to be judged on a work that was so unusual in terms of having to come in and direct these kids. I basically said I would like to give him another shot to work with adults."

In Brannon Braga's script, Picard in a Runabout come upon the Enterprise fighting a Romulan warbird....both frozen in time. Once onboard they have to figure out how to repair the fabric of time while also avoiding death and destruction for the Enterprise. "I think this is the longest optical memo we have ever had," said David Livingston of the sheet delineating all of the show's complicated visual effects. "It's over six pages long. Adam was very specific about what he wanted and I knew he was going to do great on it. He's got good genes."

"It was very different," said director Adam Nimoy of the visual effects intensive episode which required several additional days of blue-screen work after wrapping principal photography to depict the Enterprise and Romulan ship's personnel frozen in time. "I relied a lot on the special effects guys in

STAR TREK
THE NEXT GENERATION™

THE ROMULAN PRIZE

THE NEW NOVEL BY SIMON HAWKE

POCKET
BOOKS
STAR TREK®
79746•8

In a similar vein to this Next Generation *novel, "Timescape" had the* Enterprise *and a Romulan Warbird frozen in time (novel cover copyright © 1993 Pocket Books).*

they were there and I was there asking them questions just like with everyone else. They know that I am inquisitive, interested and fascinated by what they do and that I really want to come out with a product that is satisfying. It's not a question of me going and sitting in a closed room and blocking all this stuff out and then meeting with them on the set and saying, 'Can I do this?' I want to know now what the parameters are so that I'm very well prepared, as well prepared as I can be, by the time we get there, and that we're in synch. We had a lot of optical meetings in an attempt to work out exactly how the logistics would work to make scenes pay off."

"This is 'Cause & Effect' times ten," said Brannon Braga, referring to his fifth season teleplay involving the Enterprise's destruction while trapped in a temporal loop. "Time is not only looping, it's moving backwards, accelerating and stopping and moving slowly. The premise is that time/space has been shattered like a windshield and caught in the middle of the shatter effect is the Enterprise and a Romulan warbird in mid-battle. Picard, Data, Troi and Geordi have to figure out what happened and they walk around a scene of time being frozen. We have to figure out

an attempt to keep what I thought was the drama of the scene and deal with the restrictions that special effects put on you in terms of what you can do with the actors while also using those effects to maximum dramatic capacity to make it work with the scene. It's a whole different mindset. I'm learning a lot from these guys. I've known these special effects guys from last season as well because what happened by looking at pictures of still scenes and things that are actually moving very slowly. I knew the show was impossible to produce. As I was writing it, I was thinking there's no way. There's a great shot where Beverly's been phasered and you see the blast coming out through her back and we have to save her. It was very complex. There's a lot of tech but hopefully I made it clear. Visually, I think it's one of the most interesting shows. I'm fascinated by doing time travel shows that aren't the typical time travel shows. What's most interesting about time manipulation is the way we perceive time and time travel in small increments, matter of minutes or hours. The big time travel shows are fascinating too but so little has been done with other time travel stories which have much more potential."

Richard James and his production team built the living quarters for the Runabout, the warp-speed shuttle established in DS9. The wonderful new set will become a standing set on TNG's sister series. "DS9 had the cockpit already for the interior and this script called for the living quarters of the Runabout," said James. "We built it in record time. We had five days to do it and to develop the interior of a ship. Unfortunately, this is one area

where you want to get into detail since it's like a yacht or an airplane where it's really customized. We tried to accomplish that on the Runabout and the crew did an excellent job in very little time."

Episode #152
"Descent"

Teleplay by Ron Moore
Story by Jeri Taylor
Directed by Alexander Singer

Guest Starring:
John Neville (Isaac Newton), Jim Norton (Albert Einstein), Natalija Nogulich (Admiral Nechayev), Brian J. Cousins (Crosis), Professor Stephen Hawking (Himself)

The Borg return to menace the Federation as vicious, individualistic killing machines. During this battle, Data experiences his first emotion: anger and subsequently pleasure after killing one of the metamorphosed automotons. After Data flees the ship with one of the captured Borg warriors, the Enterprise pursues his shuttlepod to an unexplored planet where the Away Team finds Data paired up with his evil brother, Lore, as the leader of the once mass-totality.

• • • •

"Descent" boasts a delightful teaser in which Stephen Hawking guests stars along with an irascible star turn by BARRON MUNCHAUSEN's John Neville as

Sir Isaac Newton. Hawking, 51, who is author of the bestselling book, "A Brief History Of Time," is the Lucasian Professor of Mathematics at Cambridge University, a chair once held by Isaac Newton. His theories on black holes cast doubt on whether the big bang theory was correct and his research has addressed such subjects as the origin of the universe and the unified theory of space and time. Hawking, who was diagnosed with a motor neuron disorder, better known as Lou Gehrig's disease, is confined to a wheelchair and has lost the ability to speak. He uses a finger to communicate by punching commands into a voice synthesizer.

Visiting Stage 8 while at Paramount to promote the video release of Errol Morris' film, "A Brief History Of Time," which chronicled Hawking's life and work, the world-renowned physicist startled people when he made a very unorthodox request through his touch-keypad.

Recalled Rick Berman, "I got a phone call that Stephen Hawking was outside Stage 8 and wanted to come in and see the STAR TREK sets and was it okay? Of course, I immediately said yes and headed down to the soundstage. I was introduced and asked him if he'd like to see some more of the sets and he, with his computerized voice synthesizer, said he would. When we got to the bridge of the Enterprise, he started punching in something that he was going to say to us. He just moves one thumb and with it he has a computerized monitor that has a dictionary of various word groups so that he can construct sentences and then they eventually come out as a synthesized voice from the computer. After about 60 seconds of punching this little button, out of the computer came a sentence that I will never forget, and it was, 'Would you lift me out of my chair and put me into the Captain's seat?' It was a pretty amazing sight to have perhaps the greatest mind of the latter half of the 20th Century in Applied Mathematics and Theoretical Physics wanting more than anything else at that moment to sit in Picard's chair."

Even more surprising to Berman was the call he received the next day from his friend, Leonard Nimoy, who had been at the Hawking video premiere party the evening before. He told Berman that the professor had expressed a desire to be on STAR TREK. "The next day I called his people and it turned out that he was interested and with the help of Ron Moore, we came up with an idea for a scene where Data goes to the

The Borg returned, this time with an attitude, and threatened the entire Federation in the sixth season cliffhanger, "Descent" (comic cover copyright © 1993 DC Comics)

Holodeck to play a little poker and he conjures up images of Sir Isaac Newton, Albert Einstein and Hawking," said Berman. "We told Hawking that we wanted him to give us some notes on the script and he did and he said that he loved it and agreed to do it."

For the season cliff-hanger, NEXT GENERATION once again ventured off the lot to shoot. "We were looking for a building in which eventually the Borg will appear and we found a location that worked for us," said Berman. "I have to get used to the fact Richard has done this for years and has very strong ideas and very clearly stated ideas and he'll try to get me anything I want. All that I really require is that he's on a level of understanding as quickly as I am and will and covert it into film and that he thinks of himself as a film-maker and he does."

One day of the eight day shoot took place in Simi Valley at the Brandies Institute where STAR TREK VI had shot it's climatic Khitomer Conference scenes. "We're also did a Borg hall that the Borg took over," said Richard James. "It's a civilization that they have taken over and the architecture is not really representative of the Borg. They've added their own touches which include the floor design and some banners that we hung up. There were a couple of instances where location would have been nice. It opens up the scope of the show. This year it didn't seem to have that."

Surprisingly, Rick Berman is not as keen on the Borg as many of the fans who have extolled them as TREK's best villain ever. Said Berman, "I find them very two-dimensional in a way. They are faceless characters without personality and without specific character traits. They're sort of a one-beat group of bad guys to me. In 'Best of Both Worlds' they represented a threat as opposed to characters, and that was a great episode. In 'I, Borg' you had the antithesis of that fact, which was a Borg pulled away from the collective and was made human. It turned into a character and was given a personality and something to be sympathetic towards. My only interest in Borg is when they're used off center in other than the way they were originally conceived. In 'Descent', we have a story that is using the Borg in a different way and I think quite effectively. It's going to be part II before it gets resolved, because there's very little of them in Part One."

"We were toying with the idea of the Enterprise being called to be reassigned as a flagship, kind of Queen Marry type of thing and everyone was going to be dispersed to different postings," said Brannon Braga of one of the original ideas for the cliffhanger. "It would have basically been the dismantling of the Enterprise, but people weren't responding to that so we came up with the Borg show. I think it's so good and dark and sinister. This is Data's descent into violent tendencies and anger and hostility and the Borg and Lore's return. It's very dark. Frequently we will allude to classic films to get started and it always evolves in a new direction. In this case, HEART OF DARKNESS was an idea we had. The most compelling thing to me about this episode, aside from the fact that Data is exploring his dark side, is that the first emotion he thinks he feels is anger and that Lore has become this maniac. He's come to a point where he does not want any part of his biological past, he feels the machine life form is the perfect life form and, of course, Lore holds tremendous appeal to the Borg. He's out to eradicate all organic life forms and the superior life form must prevail. It's an interesting genocidal metaphor. Lore is Hitler and the Borg are the Nazis. He's changed them — and now he's found a way to get Data back by tapping into his ethical program. It's a great idea."

"It's pretty fucking dark," agreed Ron Moore. "They're just killers now and they don't care about your technology. Now they don't want to assimilate you, they just want to kill you. That's their whole drive. That is just so horrible. There was a lot of nice stuff in 'Best of Both Worlds' and it's the big act to follow. People expect a lot out of Borg shows. They've changed and they haven't changed for the better. After you go up the river, there's real heavy shit at the end of the cliffhanger."

The HEART OF DARKNESS allusion was not lost on anyone, including Jeri Taylor who points to Lore as a Kurtzian type of character in the piece. "In a very loose way, we sort of kept calling it 'Up the River' and we talked about the idea that there was this mysterious figure behind the Borg. We did not want to bring the

Borg back just to do another one and nothing came along for quite awhile. One of the early incarnations of the season ender involved a new race of villains, since we figured we needed some fresh blood. But Ron Moore mentioned the Borg and the idea that they've changed, and somehow it all fell together with Lore and opened up. If you leave things alone, at the right moment they rise up of their own accord and jump in your lap.

It's Lore's ethnic cleansing, if you will, which is the tact we're taking on it. That is the villainous aspect of it and, ultimately, the brothers having to deal with each other in that sort of mythic slaying of the evil brother."

••••

APPENDIX

QUESTION & ANSWER SESSION

"STAR TREK: THE NEXT GENERATION"

January 13, 1993

PRESENT:

Brent Spiner, Gates McFadden, Jonathan Frakes, Jeri Taylor, Michael Miller, Rick Berman, Patrick Stewart, LeVar Burton, Marina Sirtis, Michael Dorn.

INTRODUCTION:

I won't take too much time by telling you about all the achievements of "Star Trek: The Next Generation." I think everything that needs to be said has been said already — the phenomenal success that this show has enjoyed since it premiered in September of 1987. So I will get right to introducing our producers and our cast members for you. Two gentlemen whom you met earlier, the executive producers of "Star Trek: The Next Generation," Rick Berman and Michael Piller; our co-executive producer, Jeri Taylor; Captain Jean Luc Picard, Patrick Stewart; Commander William Riker, Jonathan Frakes; Lieutenant Commander Geordie La Forge, LeVar Burton; Lieutenant Worf, Michael Dorn; Dr. Beverly Crusher, Gates McFadden; Counselor Deanna Troi, Marina Sirtis; and Lieutenant Commander Data, Brent Spiner.

Q: I have a question for Mr. Berman. Will there be a "Next Generation" film? Are there plans in the works along that, and if so, is there a sort of finite limit on how long you'll be staying in first run series?

RICK BERMAN:
Yes, there are definitely plans underfoot for a "Next Generation" feature film. As to when it's going to be....

Q: Is there a target date?

RICK BERMAN:
I don't believe there is a target date right at the moment, and as far as how much more "Next Generation" there's going to be, there is certainly envisioning a seventh season beyond the present sixth season, and beyond that who knows?

Q: To the actors, and to follow up on that as far as how much of the cast will be there, I understand, Mr. Stewart, you have already decided not to come back for the seventh season, is that right? Are there any other actors who have decided they won't be coming back for the next season? Let me ask Mr. Stewart first to make sure I'm sure.

PATRICK STEWART:
You understand wrong.

Q: Oh, okay. Tell us, will you definitely be back next year or are you still deciding?

PATRICK STEWART:
That's in negotiation.

RICK BERMAN:
The studio is presently discussing this with all the actors, so you are going to get this answer seven times over.

Q: I was wondering if the writers and also the cast members could talk about your favorite episode, the favorite one you've written and your favorite episode as performers.

MICHAEL PILLER:
Well, just very briefly, my favorite one that I had anything to do with was "Best of Both Worlds," which was the first cliffhanger we did. It had a wonderful performance by Patrick in the Borg costume, and we just reprised it. Jeri?

JERI TAYLOR:
I think the favorite one that I

Patrick Stewart: Captain Jean Luc Picard (photo copyright © 1993 Karen Witkowski).

have done is "The Outcast," which was a very controversial episode and that's why I wanted to write it. It's something I felt very close to because in many ways as a woman I feel like someone who is disenfranchised and the message of intolerance to all people who are disenfranchised and disempowered was an important one.

MICHAEL DORN:
Actually I have two that are tied for my favorite, and interestingly enough Jonathan directed both of them. He directed "The Drumhead" and "The Offspring", when Data builds a child. But those two are my favorites. I mean, it was a wonderful courtroom drama that could have easily been done wrong. "The Offspring"....you know, being sensitive as I am, I got very misty at the end of that, and it was a very, very lovely episode.

MARINA SIRTIS:
I have two that tie. One of them was actually the first episode of the second season, which was "The Child," and in some ways it's my very, very favorite. I think my second favorite would be "The Loss," where Troi loses her empathy. But I think "The Offspring" has got to be one of the best episodes we've ever done. You notice that the two I like the best were the ones that I'm in

the most. "The Offspring" too, I think. Oh, and Patrick's — what was that episode called where you were tortured?

PATRICK STEWART:
Life.

MICHAEL PILLER:
"Chain of Command."

PATRICK STEWART:
Part Two....."The Offspring" too was my favorite episode, which happened to be Jonathan Frakes' first direction for "The Next Generation." Directing debut, Jonathan.

JONATHAN FRAKES:
It was my directing debut.

PATRICK STEWART:
Terrific script and wonderful performances and really marvelous direction.

JONATHAN FRAKES:
My favorite episode too.

BRENT SPINER:
I didn't really care for "The Offspring."

Q: Patrick, I remember talking to you the first season. You did your one-man show, you did your Shakespearean work, but with this high profile visibility, how have things changed for you?

PATRICK STEWART:
You've been asking me this question every year for the last six years, haven't you?

Q: You've been giving me the same answers.

PATRICK STEWART:
Always the same answer. I told you, I think, three years ago, my tennis game has improved. I have just come back from several weeks in New York, and also a week on vacation, and even sitting on a Caribbean beach one cannot escape the impact that this series and the whole "Star Trek" mythology continues to have, and daily during the past month I have been overwhelmed and made extraordinarily proud to continue to be associated with a program like this, because I have been reminded every day of the continuing impact in all possible areas of what this show does. And that has been for me the most significant change in that it is associated with something that I'm very proud of.

Q: Brent, let me ask you. I wanted to ask people in general what it's like to do one of the "Star Trek" conventions. And Brent, I heard something about you were at a New York convention and someone asked a question about Data's

Jonathan Frakes: Commander William Riker (photo copyright © 1993 Karen Witkowski)

sexuality or something like that, and pretty soon the audience started shouting at each other instead of at you....

BRENT SPINER:
It's exactly like that. It evolved eventually into a mud wrestling competition. No, actually, they're very tame, really. And they're very nice. They're really an incredibly pleasant experience, to do conventions, because it's not often that you walk out to an audience of people that are nothing but positive about seeing you. I mean, worship is a hard thing to reject, you know. But they are, in general, very nice, and the people are very polite, and they're genuinely interested and excited about being there.

Q: I have a question for Gates, and whichever other cast member may care to address this. Very quietly, by the end of this season, your show will have run twice as long as the original "Star Trek" series. When you started six years ago, many people were saying, "This thing will never come up to the original series. It just won't last." And now, as I said, you're about to go twice as long as it did.

GATES MCFADDEN:
I think that when we all began, the press kept asking, "Do you

have any trepidation because of the onus of the 'Star Trek' that came before you?" And I believe — and I don't want to speak for everybody —that we all said, "No, actually, we don't feel that. This is a new show, and you sign a contract for a certain number of years and you just see what happens." I don't know what it was, but the was a certain point when we realized there was a very good chance this was going to run the full six years of our contract, and, personally, the six years have gone very quickly. A lot has happened. All of us are busy all the time and often doing other things, and so I think my reflection is going to come later. Right now, it's still in a whirlwind and there are still friends of mine who say, "Oh, it's still on? I haven't even seen it yet." So there are people out there who still haven't seen it, and yet I'm told that we're more popular than ever. And it's just now being seen in many of the European countries and I'm not sure where else in the world. So, it was fun. I was just in London and people were just beginning to watch several seasons ago. So they're going, "Oh, tell us what happens next." And you're like, "Oh, babe, you're like years behind." So I don't know.

Q: Patrick, in the first episode of "Deep

Space", you seemed not to want to apologize for your experience with the Borg when Sisko comes in. It seems like this is what happened, and he seemed like he wanted an explanation. Was that purposely done, just to leave it with no apologies necessary for what you've done to the.....

PATRICK STEWART:
You know, I really think that question should be addressed to Michael and Jeri, as they were primarily responsible for what I said.

MICHAEL PILLER:
By the way, that was not Patrick, it was Picard who felt that way. I don't know. It seems to me that the things that Rick and I talked about at that point in time are that that happened, that essentially Picard was taken off and raped by the Borg and that nobody holds Picard responsible. For Sisko to have come and sort of confronted him was something that was totally inappropriate in that situation for Sisko to do. And how the captain responded to that was, you know, to be contained and reluctant to engage him in any conflict because he was sympathetic with the fellow, but at the same time he was a little bit worried about him because of the way he's coming on in that situation. So, that's really

Michael Dorn: Security Chief Worf (photo copyright © 1993 Karen Witkowski).

where the origins are.

PATRICK STEWART:
Actually, you know, we dealt largely with that in the episode that followed the Borg episodes, in one called "Family" where that question of responsibility and guilt was dealt with intensively.

Q: Did Gene Roddenberry ever put his arm around any of you and say, "OK, this is what I envision" or have a heart-to-heart about your character or the show. Michael, would you start?

MICHAEL DORN:
It's funny, when I got the job and before I started filming, I went up to Gene and I said, "What do you want from this character? What do you envision? Who is he?" And, once again, one of the nicest things or smartest things or great things for an actor to hear, he said, "Forget everything that you've seen or heard or read or anything about Klingons, and just make it your own," and I said, "Great." That's like nirvana, to be able to just go ahead and build a character from the ground up. It's very funny. I don't really envision him as being gone. I mean, he is gone, I know that. But it's sort of like he was there and he's not there, but he isn't gone. He's just kind of like still

hanging out there. I still see him around the studios. I come here late at night sometimes....

Q: Have all of you collected those "Next Generation" action figures?

MARINA SIRTIS:
Actually, I'm going to answer this one, because we finally got a toy doll this year, with movable parts. It was great. Not removable parts. I have to say, it's actually amazing to have a doll of you, even though it doesn't really look like you. I mean, I think we'd all agree that they're not exactly great likenesses. The body is great. I approve of the body 100%. But it is weird. I got it this weekend, and it's kind of sitting there in a drawer, and every time I open the drawer I see it, and there it is forever. We sold more dolls I think at the convention in San Diego this weekend than any other product. I was signing them all afternoon. So they're obviously successful. It's just really weird to be represented that way, as an action figure, with your little compact and portable computer and stuff.

Q: I've got a question for the producers. I've noticed that the first, second and third highest rating sin the history of "Next Generation"

was when you brought original "Star Trek" characters back. Do you have any plans to resurrect any other characters, or maybe bring Spock back for an appearance?

RICK BERMAN:
William Shatner it going to be a regular in the seventh season. We're always discussing that with the actors on the original series. We need logical ways to bring them back. We do our best to do that. In our pilot five and a half years ago, we had Dr. McCoy, who was well over 200 years old, or close to it. And Spock we could bring back because Vulcans live a long time. And Scotty we could bring back because someone came up with this clever idea about him being put in a transporter loop and sort of hanging in suspended animation for 70 years. It'll take another idea like that to bring one of the other actors back. They're all quite anxious and willing to come back if the right script comes back.

Q: Michael, over here. I was wondering, the other actors are probably pretty readily recognized. I'm wondering if you experienced the same kind of recognition factor, because since you wear make-up all the time, your voice is very distinctive. I'm sure that

Marina Sirtis: Counselor Deanna Troi (photo copyright © 1993 Karen Witkowski).

many people don't really know what you look like.

MICHAEL DORN:
The funny thing is that it's one of the good and bad aspects of the character, of playing the character, because....90% of it is good because I love the anonymity. I went away on vacation and was in this place for eight days and nobody recognized me at all until the last day, and somebody happened to have a "Star Trek" book, some kind of guide book with my picture, my regular picture, and they kind of spread through the hotel where I was that I was there. And that was nice. But the 10% is basically, if you're on a show that's really successful and does really well, you kind of at times would like to be recognized for that. Sometimes, "Hey, you do a great job" or "We love the show" or whatever the case may be, would be nice. But I'd say it's 90% not 10% that I enjoy the anonymity.

Q: Mr. Stewart, very early in your "Star Trek" career we had a conversation in which you talked with considerable amazement about having had an intelligent conversation with some lizard people, and I wondered if you'd learned to love lizard people and how this has affected your world view.

PATRICK STEWART:
Well, since the lizard people many things have changed around here. I've had intelligent conversations with oil slicks. It's commonplace amongst the cast that we continually remind ourselves of the reality of what we're engaged in, that for example we can — all of us, as we did in one episode — stand around and talk to an oil slick, and it's vital to the way the show operates that there would seem nothing unusual or strange about this ever under any circumstances, because fundamentally it is putting out the message that difference is to be celebrated and not to be feared or mocked or attacked in any way. It's one of the fundamental tenets of this show. Although we make fun of it....

MICHAEL DORN:
I was going to say, we had those looks. After the scene's over, we looked at each other, "I'm talking to an oil slick here. Twenty years with RSC, I'm talking to an oil slick."

PATRICK STEWART:
Well, we say, "That's very 'Star Trek.'"

Q: Did the holodeck evolve from the virtual reality that's beginning to be experimented with today, or did it sort of spring forth entirely as a completely new technology in the future, in the 24th century?

RICK BERMAN:
Gene Roddenberry came up with the idea of the holodecks, and we've met a lot of virtual reality people who I think get a lot of their creative ideas from the holodecks, so I think it's life imitating art in a sense.

Q: For the producers, writers and actors, in the sixth year does this show still offer challenges? Are there things you haven't really examined?

MARINA SIRTIS:
I think that there are still a lot of aspects of my character that we haven't — I'll just speak for my character — that we haven't explored. Talking of the Holodeck, you've never seen what Troi does on the holodeck. We've never seen her really in an off-duty situation where she's just hanging out. What does she do? I think there's a lot of stuff for each of us that we haven't really delved into, and as Patrick I think said, and he used it as a bit of advice I think in an interview one time, and I have taken it myself now, and that is to find something new in every episode that you haven't done before, and find something

Gates McFadden: Dr. Beverly Crusher (photo copyright © 1993 Karen Witkowski).

new for your character in every episode, and I think that's a good piece of advice. Ever since I've heard it, I've definitely been following it. So I don't think there is. I mean, would you ask the guys over at "Cheers" the same question? They've been on for 12 years and they're still coming up with great new.... I still laugh out loud at that show. So, I don't think that's necessarily the case.

Q: A quick question for LeVar. Yesterday we all interviewed the people on "Queen", Alex Hailey's last book, and I wondered whether there was an opportunity for you to be in that or are you died down contractually with "Next Generation" not to be able to do it.

LEVAR BURTON:
No, our producers on "Next Generation" are incredible about allowing us the freedom whenever possible to go and engage in other projects. "Queen" was a situation where David Wolper had made a conscious decision not to have anybody from the original "Roots" cast in "Queen". That was what he told me. But I just saw that Madge Sinclair is a member of the cast, so there you go, there's the integrity of David Wolper right there on a platter for you.

BRENT SPINER:
What we said was no one who played Kunte Kinte would be in "Queen."

LEVAR BURTON:
Thanks a lot, Brent.

Q: Gates and Marina, when the reviews for "Deep Space Nine" came out, a lot of writers latched on to the fact that it seemed to mark an empowerment for women in the "Star Trek" saga, that they wee taking over the ship and Sisko was gone. And I couldn't help but wonder how the two of you reacted to that, if you saw any of those kinds of reviews. Do you feel that your characters have been allowed to stand on equal footing with the male characters?

GATES MCFADDEN:
Sometimes they have and sometimes they haven't. I think that there is a ways to go in terms of our show. I certainly know that I've been — I think my producers would vouch for this — quite forthright in asking for more of that all the time. I know that Marina and I always laughed about the fact that both of us can do fencing and that sort of thing, yet we're the ones who bash the pots over the warriors' heads, instead of doing our karate, or whatever. I do think we've had a ways to go. I personally love

going on the Away Team missions and would love to do more of them. I haven't seen "Deep Space." I was out of the country and I haven't seen that, nor have I seen the reviews. But I have heard this.

RICK BERMAN:
You sound like Bill Shatner saying, "I've never seen 'The Next Generation.'"

GATES MCFADDEN:
Well, it's only been a week.

MARINA SIRTIS:
It's only been on two weeks.

GATES MCFADDEN:
So I would like to see that. If that's true, I'm sure all of that suffragette will just sort of trickle down to our show. If we can catch the drippings, that would be great.

MARINA SIRTIS:
I think there's a difference. And the fundamental difference is that the two female officers in "Deep Space Nine" are a science officer and a Bajoran major who is second in command of the space station. The two female characters on "Next Generation" are a doctor and a psychologist, and as such you're kind of limited as to what you can do with a doctor and a psychologist.

LeVar Burton: Chief Engineer Geordi LaForge (photo copyright © 1993 Karen Witkowski).

GATES MCFADDEN:
I'm second ranking officer. I've got his rank.

MARINA SIRTIS:
But you're not. You're not second in command. Jonathan is. Kira is the second in command. It's a slightly different thing. Yes, the doctor can dispose of the captain if he's being bad. But Kira....they have different ranks. And we have said to our producers why can't we do this, and when they say a doctor and a psychologist, especially the psychologist — I'm speak for me because the doctor isn't so bad — but for a psychologist who's basically a peaceful analytical kind of a person, it doesn't really fit. But after saying that, there is an episode coming up this season where I am kidnapped by the Romulans, or where Troi is kidnapped by the Romulans, and she kicks some major butt. So, it can happen, but it's kind of....when we're taken over by entities, and stuff like that, as opposed to our real characters. But good for them on "Deep space." I think it's great that they're actually going forward.

JERI TAYLOR:
I'd like to get in on this and say that we are as producers and writers — and I particularly am very aware of the problem — I think they're both

right. Gene gave the women on the show the role of nurturers and care-givers, which is in many ways appropriate but it is limiting. It's hard for us at times to....it becomes a strain to put those people in situations where they can show their stuff. But we have a couple of shows coming up and one that Marina just mentioned ["Face of the Enemy"]. She's a very, very formidable tough person in a scary and dangerous situation.

PATRICK STEWART:
Historically, the fact is that when the series was created, there was another female character and if Denise Crosby had chosen to stay with the series instead of asking to leave, we would still have a woman as head of security doing the job that Worf does now. And I've often wondered that if that had remained the case, what a difference that would have made to Marina and Gates' characters, if you had had a woman in that particular position. My feeling is it would have changed the female dynamics throughout the entire series. And although I think on the whole Michael [Dorn] is doing quite a good job, I enjoyed having Denise Crosby around. I think I've said too much.

MICHAEL PILLER:
You lied to me.

PATRICK STEWART:
No, Michael, you wanted me to lie to you.

Q: Jonathan, is there a feeling on your part of kind of like the holder of the vice presidency, where you.....do you know what I'm getting at?

JONATHAN FRAKES:
Yes, I know just what you're getting at. I suppose that's the case. I like to think of myself more like Al Gore than Dan Quayle.

Q: How do you flush that out, though? Obviously the participation that you've had in this show is critical to the show.

JONATHAN FRAKES:
Whenever the captain leaves the bridge, I sit in his chair. The character I play runs the away teams, I'm sure it says in some bio somewhere. He's full of daring do, it says in the bio somewhere as well.

Q: Marina mentioned that the Romulans are going to get a little feisty in the near future. Do you have anything special planned for the February and May sweeps?

JERI TAYLOR:
Yes we do, but it would be unfair to spoil the surprise for

Brent Spiner: Science Officer Data (photo copyright © 1993 Karen Witkowski).

you. Yes, we try to pack for the sweeps and that is one of the episodes that we have upcoming. We have a marvelous two-parter with Worf, Michael Dorn, that I think is an extremely emotional, wrenching kind of two episodes. So, we try to heighten some of our favorite characters, bring an added kind of....there's more production value in some of those too. We always try to do our best and do good stories every time. I think we give a little more panache to some of the sweep shows.

Q: When I saw "Deep Space Nine"....you can read too much into these things, but I sort of saw a cold war analogy to that — the Russian Empire breaking up, you had an alien empire sort of breaking up by the space station. I'm just wondering if there are cold war analogies to the future as you design these different conflicts between the different races and nations.

MICHAEL PILLER:
Well, you know, anything you see on "Deep Space Nine" and "Next Generation" affect one another. One of the advantages of setting both series in the same time period is that we're drawing from the same universe. So the kinds of things that are happening with the Cardassians allow us to build those characters in new and unique ways. What we had just before "Deep Space Nine" was this marvelous two-parter with this whole incursion business that the Cardassians were doing that ultimately led to the capture of Picard, and an episode if you didn't see it featured what I believe is Patrick Stewart's best performance that I've ever seen in the history of this show, and one that I hope is certainly considered at Emmy time. It gives us an opportunity to explore inter-character relationships, interracial relationships, with the Cardassians, and I'm sure that things that happened with the Romulans and the Klingons will also affect development of stories in the future.

RICK BERMAN:
I think you can't escape cold war analogies in any "Star Trek." I think dating all the way back to the original series there have been cold war analogies continually running through everything having to do with "Star Trek."

Q: Jeri, Whoopi's appearances on the show are marvelous. Will we be seeing more or less of her?

JERI TAYLOR:
We will see as much of Whoopi as we can. It's really her schedule that precludes any more of her. She's been very, very busy doing her talk show, and so she was taken out of the running for a number of months. And she wants to do the show. She loves the show, and she recently told us that she wants to come back, gave us a window of opportunity, and so we immediately planned and structured a show that has her in it. So you will be seeing her again. As much as she is available to us, we will fit her in.

Q: Mr. Stewart, they're talking some about not getting the Emmys in the past and so forth. I just wanted to ask, as much as the whole thing about "good work is its own reward" and so forth, has this sometimes kind of hurt your feelings in the past when you didn't get the nominations, and beyond this year's episode about the torture and so forth, were there a few episodes in the past where afterwards you thought, "Well, that was a particularly great role, I just really loved doing that episode."

PATRICK STEWART:
No, it hasn't hurt my feelings at all. It has absolutely infuriated me and enraged me when I see my colleagues in every department — and I've never quite seen the point of separating creative from tech-

nical — being overlooked for the work that they do, for the show itself, for the writing, for the performance, and for direction. I find it incomprehensible that for five straight years the show should have gone utterly unrecognized in all of those categories.

Q: Do you think that has something to do with science fiction not being taken seriously as well as the educational aspects. In literature, science fiction is something of a second class citizen, sometimes unfairly.

RICK BERMAN:
I think there could be some truth in that. I think that we have a number of strikes against us, onuses that have hung on over these five and a half years, and one is that it's a syndicated show and another is that it's science fiction, and another is that it's a sequel. And I think, as Michael said before, that the major of those is the fact that it's a syndicated show, at least in terms of its recognition among the creative community that votes for things like Emmy Awards.

Q: Did Gene leave a bible for this show? Are you still working off that, or is everything that's happening with the show now new?

RICK BERMAN:
Well, the bible was written before our first episode and it was continually updated and changed. These characters have all found themselves over the last six years and new mythology and nomenclature has developed over those years. But, no, Gene did not leave a master plan that's sitting somewhere that we draw from, but he did leave in all of us a feeling of what he wanted "Star Trek" to be and I think we've all done our best to stay true to that.

Q: For the producers, when you begin hiatus on both your programs, what are your professional plans?

JERI TAYLOR:
There is no hiatus for the producers. These actors get 10 or 11 weeks off. By the time we're done cutting the last episode, we're already in prep on the first one of the next season. So, if we can steal a couple of weeks, we're lucky.
RICK BERMAN: I had one week last year. Stories are hard to come by for these shows. They're very, very hard to come by. It's a story-driven series. We are constantly scratching and searching and looking, and if you took a month off, which many people on series do, we would be so far behind we would never be

able to go into production. So there just is no time for anything but this.

MICHAEL PILLER:
On top of that, we do 26, which I don't know of any network — ours certainly —that do that. Maybe some comedies do. But coming up with 26 shows a year doesn't give much time for rest.

Q: For the cast, is there any aspect of your characters that you haven't gotten a chance to explore yet that you would like to explore in future episodes?

MICHAEL DORN:
I must have been very lucky that they sort of....I mean, Worf has been really busy. He had a mate, lost her, has a son, and he has adoptive parents, and real parents that were killed, and he was paralyzed for a while. I've been very fortunate where they have touched on a lot of Worf's character. So, I'm probably one of the most fortunate ones.

LEVAR BURTON:
I think, finally, in this season we have gotten around to addressing a real gaping hold in Geordi's life. We completed an episode before the holidays where he falls in love with a real live human being, not a holographic representation

from the holodeck, and I'm real pleased about that.

PATRICK STEWART:
Similarly, yes, my feeling is that whereas two or three seasons ago I might have been complaining about being too much of a desk captain, a briefcase captain. My body count has risen dramatically in the last few episodes.

RICK BERMAN:
Wait until next week. We kill at least 15 people next week.

PATRICK STEWART:
I've been seriously hurting people for about two years now, and that's given me deep satisfaction. Also, they addressed the romantic, the real living romantic side of Picard. Perhaps if there's one area which I would personally enjoy because it gives me a lot of pleasure and I haven't had much of it in the past, is the humorous, ironic, wittier side of our good captain.

JONATHAN FRAKES:
Irony. We need more irony. We've been begging for irony. I know it's not easy to write. What happened to the Riker-Troi relationship?

GATES MCFADDEN:
What Riker-Troi relationship? Well, I could say the same thing, Picard-Crusher, my dar-

ling captain. You left that out.

PATRICK STEWART:
That's the one thing that significantly has been left out. Gates, don't cry. I hate it when you cry.

GATES MCFADDEN:
We do have breakfast together, I suppose. I would like to see that, and then, you know, more humor. Pratfalls on the deck, I'm all for that.

PATRICK STEWART:
Actually it's true, I do feel the loss of that special relationship that was developing in the first season between the doctor and the captain, and that there was much more still to be mined in that area. Brent?

BRENT SPINER:
I'm sorry, was the question who did I want to have a relationship with? I've lost track. No, it had something to do with exploration of the character, right? Because, frankly, I'd like to have a relationship with anyone at this point. Actually, I feel very fortunate to have been selected initially to play this part. It's been a really sweet part to play and I've gotten to do about 15 other characters along the way, and they've opened up every part of my body at this point, save one, and we're going to save that one I think, for a sweeps,

probably. I think Michael and Rick did a great job of enhancing Gene's imagination and where he wanted to take the character and I think Jeri's doing a terrific job this season in the same way. I've done things this year I have never done in the five previous years, and I'm sure that will continue until, you know, there probably is a fail-safe of some sort if we'd stop being creative her. I think I explode, basically, is what happens.

PATRICK STEWART:
You know, actually, there has been quite a significant change in the experience for all of us this year, which is because Michael and Rick necessarily have been having to divide their time between us and "Deep Space Nine". But all of us therefore have had much more working creative contact with Jeri Taylor than we've had before. And, not only has there been an absolute continuity of work, but that those occasions when I along with other actors have been working alongside Jeri, it has been incredibly stimulating — Jeri — and very satisfying, and you've had a fantastic year, I think.

Q: Jeri, could you tell us a little bit more about that, since you hear a lot about the fact that more of the names in creating science fiction tend to be male than female. Tell us a little bit about your roots. You started to be interested in sci fi at what age? What got you here? And if you're becoming ad hoc in charge of this show because you're getting those two guys out of the way. Are you surprised by being where you are in "Star Trek"?

JERI TAYLOR:
Yes, very much so. When I first came on staff three years ago, I was a "Star Trek" virgin. I had not seen any of the original series, any of this series, or any of the movies. I knew nothing about this world. I knew very little about science fiction. I had read some as a child, but it was completely foreign ground to me. I had a track record as a

writer in television and people, the human condition, emotions, character. That is my bailiwick, and fortunately under Rick and Michael that was the guiding principle of "Star Trek." The science-fiction is pizzazz, but truly, these are stories which explore the human condition, and that's what is at the heart of every.....I did a crash course in "Star Trek." I watched every episode of "Next Generation", then I went back and watched every episode of the original series. They have set a standard for the show that

I am simply trying to live up to, and this has been a turning point in my life.

The "Star Trek: The Next Generation" press conference wrapped up shortly after Jeri Taylor's answer to this question.

CAPTAIN'S LOGS

THE COMPLETE TREK VOYAGES

By
Edward Gross
&
Mark A. Altman

EXPLORING DEEP SPACE

AND BEYOND

By Mark A. Altman and David Ian Solter

B⬚XTREE